The Female Voice
in Medieval Romance Lyric

American University Studies

Series II

Romance Languages and Literature
Vol. 68

PETER LANG
New York · Bern · Frankfurt am Main · Paris

Doris Earnshaw

The Female Voice
in Medieval Romance Lyric

*For Arthur Askins
with warm regards
Doris Earnshaw
October 1989*

PETER LANG
New York · Bern · Frankfurt am Main · Paris

Library of Congress Cataloging-in-Publication Data

Earnshaw, Doris.
 The female voice in medieval Romance lyric.

 (American university studies. Series II, Romance language and literature ; vol. 68)
  Bibliography: p.
  1. Romance poetry—To 1500—History and criticism. 2. Women in literature. 3. Discourse analysis, Literary. 4. Direct discourse in literature.
 I. Title. II. Series.
 PN814.E37 1988   840'.09'02   87-29727
 ISBN 0-8204-0575-2
 ISSN 0740-9257

CIP-Titelaufnahme der Deutschen Bibliothek

Earnshaw, Doris:
The female voice in medieval Romance lyric / Doris Earnshaw. — New York; Bern; Frankfurt am Main; Paris· Lang, 1988.
 (American University Studies: Ser. 2, Romance Language and Literature; Vol. 68)
 ISBN 0-8204-0575-2

NE: American University Studies / 02

© Peter Lang Publishing, Inc., New York 1988

All rights reserved.
Reprint or reproduction, even partially, in all forms such as microfilm, xerography, microfiche, microcard, offset strictly prohibited.

Printed by Weihert-Druck GmbH, Darmstadt, West Germany

To Philip W. Damon

ACKNOWLEDGMENTS

This study was begun at the same time that I was discovering and editing the work of women poets from around the world. My colleagues in Comparative Literature at the University of California, Berkeley, who shared that exciting enterprise deepened my understanding of the role of women's speech and its history in human culture. I would like to thank especially Marsha Hudson, Joanna Bankier, Deirdre Lashgari, Bridgit Connelly, Eileen Malloy, and Laura Stortoni.

I am indebted to James Monroe, Arthur Askins, and Joseph J. Duggan for their personal encouragement and in opening the field of early Romance lyric to me. Generous assistance also came from Janette Richardson, Louise George Clubb, Mary Ritchie Key, and Robin Lakoff.

Throughout the years, Philip Damon guided and inspired me to pursue _chansons de femme_ in five Romance languages from his initial suggestion to this publication. His work on Sappho indicates his understanding of my project; often he grasped the goals before I did.

I also thank Gillian Cannon at the University of California, Irvine, for her editorial and computer skills.

TABLE OF CONTENTS

Chapter 1: The Female Voice Becomes "Borrowed Speech".. 1

    The Critical Problem Redefined: From Origins to
      Dialectical Analysis 1
    The Bibliographic Situation 3
    The Concept of Voice 11
    The Dramatic Monologue: Two "Witch" Poems 15
    Modern Use of the Female Voice: Yeats, Hardy,
      and Frost 24
    Notes 29

Chapter 2: The Female Voice Determines Poetic Form .. 33

    "Double-Voiced" Speech 33
    Structures of Male Voice Response 34
    Two-Voice Lyrics 37
    The Monologue 54
    Binary Rhymes 62
    Notes 70

Chapter 3: The Persona of the Speaking Woman 75

    Mozarabic Spanish 76
    Galician-Portuguese 78
    Provençal 81
    Old French 93
    Italian 105
    Notes 115

Chapter 4: The Cultural Eccentricity of the Female
          Speaker 121

    Class Status 122
    Social Attitudes 126
    Speech Style 132
    Notes 142

Chapter 5: The Trobairitz 145

    Cansos 147
    Tensos 150
    Critical Interpretations 153
    Notes 161

Bibliography 165

Index 177

Chapter 1

> In the analysis of a speech or literary composition, nothing is more important than to determine precisely the voice or voices presented as speaking and the precise nature of the address . . . [for it] is a part of the meaning and a frame for the rest of the meaning, for the interpretation of which it supplies an indispensable control . . . .
>
> James Craig La Drière

> Remember that it is Folly and a woman who has spoken.
>
> Erasmus

THE FEMALE VOICE BECOMES "BORROWED SPEECH"

Chansons de femme, or women's songs, occupy a place of special importance in the study of medieval Romance lyric. Dating from the tenth century, they are the earliest lyrics in the vernacular languages of Western Europe. Numerically, they constitute a significant element in pre-1300 courtly literature, some 90% of the Mozarabic Spanish corpus, 34% of the Galician-Portuguese, and a diminishing but still vital part of Provençal, Old French, and Italian poetry. To many critics they have seemed, in their freshness and spontaneity of tone, an entirely new voice in Western poetry, utterly different from what one might set as their models in Greek and Latin lyric. Charmed by their supposed vivid frankness, Gaston Paris and Alfred Jeanroy spoke of them in the vocabulary of music hall entertainment. They were "charmantes bluettes" "de grâce mutine et folâtre.[1] For many generations the *chansons de femme* have brought delight to their audiences, but they have also raised difficult and controversial critical problems about their origin and place in courtly literature.

At present, two contradictory views concerning the *chansons de femme* create the need for a new interpretation of this important area of medieval lyric. One theory of long standing holds that *chansons de femme* are remnants of precourtly, oral, and traditional culture, songs of women's groups in village and manorial society. Some anonymous dance lyrics have been related to May Day festivals of pre-Christian cultures. Some songs, for example "Bele Aelis" and "Rosa Fresca Aulentissima" are found in many versions over a wide area and across several centuries. Other songs may contain references to fragments of songs; allusions which assume audience familiarity with the whole song and point to a functioning oral song tradition. We know from music anthropology that women's songs are universally a part of village life, where women have charge of rituals of birth, marriage, death, and where work is performed in groups (spinning, weaving, harvesting) accompanied by many beautiful songs. In short, critics of all the medieval Romance languages have seen the songs as survivors into written form of a pre-courtly, oral tradition.

The opposing view, that of Giuseppe Tavani, C. P. Bagley and others, is more recent and equally plausible. It sees the chansons de femme as entirely the work of the male troubadour, who sang them for the entertainment of an aristocratic audience. Whereas we have no clear proof of oral tradition in lyric, this argument contends, we do know from the manuscript chansonniers that male poets whose names are familiar wrote one, ten, or a hundred songs attributed by the anthologists. Some of the songs of a poet's repertoire may happen to be women's songs, not different from the men's love song in any important distinction. If we accept the manuscript attribution for male voice love songs, there is no reason to subtract the female voice songs from a repertoire. In the case of the courtly romances such as Guillaume de Dôle, Le Roman de Fauvel and Le Roman de la Violette, authorship of the songs found in them is clearly with the romancers since the story seems to be the prior creation. Furthermore, the presence of female personae in dramatic lyric is a long-established poetic practice of dramatists, poets, and writers of narrative from the beginning of Western literary history, hardly a new phenomenon in medieval lyric. The medieval poet merely continued the tradition of prosopopeia, the term of classical rhetoric for the adoption of a speaking voice, which may be that of a woman, or wine, water, the Cross, a talking cow, horse, cat, or fox. To assume another persona, then, was only part of the poet's craft. This interpretation, based on manuscript assignment and the rhetorical tradition, tends toward a critical judgment that would minimize differences between women's songs and the male voice love song. In fact, Cynthia Bagley concludes, from a study of the vocabulary and themes of the Galician-Portuguese man's love songs (cantigas de amor) and women's love songs (cantigas de amigo) that the only distinguishing feature is whether the address is to a lady (spoken of as senhor--lord) or to the lover (amigo--boyfriend). She writes "There is nothing else to distinguish one from another."[2]

The two conflicting interpretations of chansons de femme, the folkloric and the textually-oriented, offer a choice of two opinions: either the chansons de femme are surviving remnants of women's songs from an earlier, pre-courtly traditional society, or they are a literary mode used by the troubadour to add variety to his public performance style at court. Since these views are mutually exclusive, they call for a fresh attack from some other point of view. The present study will attempt to bring new light to these questions by reformulating the approach to the topic. The first step is, I believe, to redefine the chanson de femme or woman's song as a song with the woman's voice in all or in part of its lines. Heretofore, the term has been used vaguely to refer to supposed monologues, which, on investigation, we find covers fewer cases than one would have thought, and not any of the important groups in Mozarabic Spanish and Old French. The critical problems arise from the poet's use of the female voice as a complement to the male voice. But to discover the role and function of the female voice, we must first see its physical context. The study will, then, take as its material all lyrics in the five Romance vernacular languages of Mozarabic Spanish, Galician-Portuguese, Provençal, Old French, and Italian having, in whole or in part, lines of direct speech in a female persona. We shall further limit the study to the period bounded by Mozarabic Spanish ḫarǧas on one side and dolce stil novo on the other, that is, roughly 950-1300 A.D. In two-part lyrics (lyrics with both male and female voices) we shall examine the place and poetic function of the female voice, whether it comes at the beginning, middle, or end of the lyric. The monologue will be studied as a complementary voice within the repertoire; the range and distribution of the woman's song will be seen as it occurs in the extant poetry of a number of troubadours.

After the poetic effect of the fragmentation and incorporation of the female voice within medieval lyric has been determined, we will study the presentation of the female persona to search for common characteristics throughout Romance secular lyric. Certain patterns will emerge in the portrait of the speaking woman; in her speech, her economic and social class, and in her attitudes toward government and the church and the institution of marriage. We will stress the dialogical role of the female voice as it is used by troubadours and trouvères. Finally, questions arising from the appearance of a group of twenty trobairitz (women poets) in Provençal, alone among the Romance vernacular languages. will lead to speculation about the effect of favorable legal and political status and the influence of special qualities in the speech model of the female voice in Provençal lyric.

No collection of lyrics or reference index exists to organize the study of women's songs in medieval lyric poetry. Surviving manuscript song collections are edited and numbered, however, so that the task of checking through the total of about nine thousand songs in early Romance vernacular languages is not impossible. Only in Galician-Portuguese have anthologists and critics separated the songs (and the separation dates from medieval centuries) into three parts: songs addressed to a woman (cantigas de amor), songs addressed to a man (cantigas de amigo), and songs of scorn and invective (cantigas de escarnho e mal dizer). In other languages, anthologies such as Karl Bartsch's Altfranzösische Romanzen und Pastourellen contain many lyrics with a female persona, but anthologies may also fail to include some of the most interesting lyrics for this study, and they cannot be relied on. A thorough search of the entire corpus of Provençal, Old French, and Italian lyric would result in the discovery of important examples. The present work is based on a study of manuscripts in the Bibliothèque Nationale and the Bibliothèque de l'Arsenal in Paris, as well as in printed editions. Here I will briefly describe the locations and editions of texts that contain lyrics one or more of whose lines have direct speech in a female voice.

Although predicted and even mentioned in scholarly articles earlier, the significance of the Mozarabic Spanish lyrics was first discovered by the Hebraist Samuel Miklos Stern in 1948. They are short lyrics of two to eight lines (but most often four) in Romance meters occupying the last part of the final stanza of the strophic poem in classical Arabic called the muwashsha (or "colored belt," from the strophic form, unusual in classical Arabic poetry). The Romance lines (written, however, in Arabic characters) placed at the close of the Arabic poem are called by their Arabic name, ḫarǧa, or "exit." They are typically, in the case of Romance ḫarǧas, in a female voice, and they give a piquant, often ironic, twist to the often florid poem, which may be a love poem or a panegyric.

As more poems gradually came to light, the small corpus of twenty-two known in 1950 grew to the present total of sixty-one (1980). In addition, ninety-three predominantly Arabic ḫarǧas from Hebrew lyrics, and forty-four mixed Arabic and Romance ḫarǧas (which may have one or two words in Romance) usually, for instance, the word for mother, 'mama') have been edited and studied recently by James Monroe (1977).[3] Monroe points out that to understand the ḫarǧa intelligently, we must be able to view the entire group, since most of them reflect linguistically the mixture of the Christian, Arabic, and Hebrew cultures that obtained in Islamic Spain from the tenth to the fourteenth centuries.

Ḫarǧa scholarship begins in 1894 with a prophetic remark of M. Menéndez y Pelayo in an article on Semitic influences in Spanish literature:

> ¿Quién sabe si podrá abrirnos nuevos horizontes esa misteriosa Rhétorica y Poética de Moisés ben Ezra, que en la biblioteca Bodleyana de Oxford existe, y que, según dicen, trata no solamente de la poesía hebrea y árabe, sino también de la vulgar neolatina?[4]

Menéndez y Pelayo writes of "versos castellanos extrañamente mezclados con el texto hebreo" and gives a Spanish version of ḫarǧa 28b "Venid, fresca jovencita. ¿Quién esconde mi corazón herido?" Investigation into the Hebrew poetry of medieval Spain was continued by the Hebraist Yitzhak F. Baer in an article in Sion (1936) in which he interprets the Romance verses of Judah Halevi's poems.[5] The news of the historic discovery of a substantial body of ḫarǧas was contained in Samuel Miklos Stern's article "Les vers finaux en espagnol dans les muwaššaḥs hispano-hébraiques: une contribution à l'histoire du muwaššah et à l'étude du vieux dialecte espagnol 'mozarabe'."[6] Following this publication, critics concerned with different Romance languages (Roncaglia, Spitzer, Dronke, Frings) published articles relating the news to their readers and stressing the importance of the new dating of the earliest Romance lyrics.[7] An example of the diffusion of the discovery and its effects on a reinterpretation of Romance lyric is the article "Un siècle de plus pour la poésie espagnole" which Pierre Groult wrote for Les Lettres Romanes in 1951.[8] Groult's article was particularly important because it made clear that the idea that since very little early Spanish poetry had been documented, the Spanish people "must have no gift for lyric," had no foundation.

Various numbering systems have been employed by editors (Klaus Heger, Emilio García Gómez, and J. M. Sola-Solé) since Stern's original display. The most recent is that of Sola-Solé, whose book Corpus de poesía mozárabe (las ḫarǧas andalusies), 1973, has become the standard text.[9] The field is, however, fluid: new material appears continually in articles; and numbers of manuscripts in private hands in Spain await study.

Of the sixty-one ḫarǧas listed in the Mozarabic Spanish corpus, fifty-four are in a female voice. That extremely high percentage (some 90%) has the effect of making these early Romance lyric fragments a key part of this study. Of the group of mixed Romance, Arabic, and Hebrew ḫarǧas totalling one hundred and ninety-eight lyrics, ninety-two, or almost half, are in a female persona. This percentage is smaller that that of the Mozarabic Spanish corpus, but it is still a significant feature of the muwaššaḥa style.

The extant corpus of Galician-Portuguese lyric is known primarily through three great songbooks. It consists of 1683 songs. The fourteenth century Cancioneiro da Ajuda (siglum A), now held by the Library of the Palacio da Ajuda, near Lisbon, received its best critical edition from the German scholar Carolina Michaelis de Vasconcellos.[10]

Her work includes brief summaries of the themes of the songs. Without access to the other two major compilations, using uncollated lists of titles, she attempted a comparative index of all three songbooks, but its inaccuracies make it of little use today. Two other editions of the Cancioneiro da Ajuda have been published: a diplomatic edition by Henry H. Carter, in 1941, and an edition with preface and notes by Marques Braga, in 1945.[11]

The second songbook of Galician-Portuguese lyrics is the Colocci-Brancuti (Siglum B, housed in the Biblioteca Nacional, Lisbon). Its history in modern times begins in the Renaissance when the Italian humanist Angel Colocci (1475-1549) compiled a list of songs from a now lost original manuscript of the middle fourteenth century. This list was inserted in the manuscript copy that was made for him, and there are discrepancies in the number of titles between the original (as seen in the list) and the surviving copy. In 1880 Enrico Molteni published an edition of this manuscript, and in the years 1949-1964 a facsimile edition in eight volumes was published by Elza Paxeco Machado and José Pedro Machado.[12]

The third songbook, the so-called Cancioneiro da Vaticana, (Siglum V, housed in the Vatican Library) was edited by Ernest Monaci as Il Canzoniere portoghese della Biblioteca Vaticana (Halle, 1875). As with Siglum B, this manuscript is a sixteenth century copy of a now unknown original. Another edition, by Theophilo Braga, Cancioneiro portuguez da Vaticana, was published in Lisbon in 1878.[13] There is a modern facsimile.

As part of a concerted effort to establish a comprehensive index for the Galician-Portuguese corpus, Jean Marie D'Heur has revised the incomplete and inaccurate numberings in the recent work, Nomenclature des troubadours.[14] One thousand six hundred and eighty-three lyrics are numbered alphabetically by first line, with previous numberings in editions of the manuscripts given in chart form. The accompanying notes and observations justify D'Heur's frequent revisions of attributions.

Other works that contain important sections of the corpus are the editions of the cantigas de amor (1932) and cantigas de amigo (1928) by Manuel José Joaquim Nunes, and of the cantigas d'escarnho e de mal dizer by Manuel Rodrigues Lapa.[15] A second edition, revised and augmented, was published by Lapa in 1970. These three studies are generously provided with notes, commentaries, glossaries, and tables, and make working in this area of medieval lyric especially agreeable.

An unusual feature of the Galician-Portuguese corpus is the classification by traditional criticism of the songs into three types: men's love songs, addressed to a lady (called senhor); songs in a female voice, addressed to a lover (primarily, though there are many exceptions, he is addressed as amigo); and the male voice songs of scorn and invective. The first group, (cantigas de amor) is the largest, about 43% of the total, or 725 songs; the cantigas de amigo, the female voice songs, number 504, or 29% of the corpus; the songs of scorn and invective (cantigas de escarnho) number slightly fewer, 450, or 26% of the corpus.

In contrast to the changing bibliographic situation for medieval lyric in Mozarabic Spanish and Galician-Portuguese, the standard reference work for Provençal lyric has remained stable for fifty years. It is the Bibliographie der Troubadours by the German scholars Alfred Pillet and Henry Carstens (Halle, 1933).[16] Building on the Bibliographie Sommaire des chansonniers provençaux (1916) of Alfred Jeanroy and subsequent work by Anglade, Monaci, Haskell, and Crescini, Pillet and Carstens provided descriptions of the more than eighty manuscripts containing lyrics in Provençal. These manuscripts are scattered throughout Europe. The list of songs includes all known manuscripts, with first line, author's name, manuscript provenance, editions, and, in the case of the major troubadours, scholarly articles. Songs from the courtly Romances are included. Women's songs are not marked as such, and can only be found by reading the text of each poet's songs. A projected publication in one edition of all Old Provençal lyrics, begun in Barcelona, has been at a standstill for a number of years. The lyrics of the trobairitz are contained in late thirteenth and early fourteenth-century manuscripts, many of which were made originally in Italy, but are now housed in Paris and Rome, for the most part.

The basic work in Old French lyric is Gaston Raynaud's two-volume Bibliographie des chansonniers français des XIIIème et XIVème siècles (Paris, 1884), revised by Hans Spanke as G. Raynaud's Bibliographie des altfranzösischen Liedes (Leiden, 1955).[17] In 1880, while Raynaud was working on an edition of Thibaud de Navarre, he gathered together all the thirteenth and fourteenth-century song collections then available in order to settle questions of attribution. During the course of this effort, which occupied him for eight years, he compiled a general list of French lyrics by manuscript and author, and published this list as Volume One of the Bibliographie. As Volume Two, he published another list of the song titles arranged by the end rhymes of the first lines. In all, Raynaud catalogued songs from twenty-eight manuscripts, fourteen of which belong to the Bibliothèque Nationale in Paris. Some are handsome works with illuminations and musical notation; ms. 5198 of the Bibliothèque de l'Arsenal, for instance, is extremely beautiful.

Raynaud's classification by rhyme groups (Volume Two of the *Bibliographie*) begins with the large patterns of endings (-a, -age, -ai, -aie, -aigne, -ain, etc.) of the last word of the first line of the lyric. The poems are then grouped within the rhyme category alphabetically by the last word of the first line (achever, agreer, aler, amer, blasmer, botoner, celer, chanter, etc.). An accompanying list of the poets' names with the placement number allows readers to make the identification of poet and poem. This system is not entirely easy to use, but with some diligence the researcher can find the place of a given lyric in the catalogue. Variations in spelling make for difficulties in using the *Bibliographie*, since Raynaud regularized spelling to conform to the French of the Ile-de-France of the thirteenth century. I believe a thorough search in both the Provençal and Old French lyric corpus would profit our understanding of the female voice in medieval Romance lyric. Some noteworthy poems might incidentally be brought to light.

Raynaud's catalogue, while a great step forward in the study of Old French lyric, was never intended to be definitive. Raynaud himself admitted so, although the work contains 2,130 titles from 223 poets. Comparison with the Pillet/Carstens *Bibliographie* for Provençal lyric reveals major differences in at least two areas of interest to this study. First, "Anonymous" has completely disappeared, whereas attributions to "anon" in Provençal number two hundred and fifty-one lyrics. Second, the presence of women troubadours has almost disappeared. There is one song by Une Dame, another by La Dame du Fayel, and two by La Duchesse de Lorraine.

Thirty years after the Raynaud *Bibliographie* was published, Alfred Jeanroy issued a supplement, his *Bibliographie sommaire des chansonniers français du moyen âge* (Paris, 1916, reprint, 1974). Jeanroy had not found any new manuscripts, but he brought the list of editions up to date and corrected entries for one hundred and eighty-two individual poems, showing that they were duplicates, or attributed incorrectly, or that their genre designation was mistaken. Jeanroy gave much attention to the question of women's songs, in this work as in his other writings. In his 1955 revision, Spanke incorporated the 1921 publications of Gennrich, and an earlier catalogue of manuscripts by E. Schwan (Berlin, 1886), numbering the lyrics from 1 to 2130a, adding to the entries a metrical analysis, short typological designations, and references to musical settings where they exist.

In 1979 Romance Monographs published Robert White Linker's *A Bibliography of Old French Lyrics*, the successor to Raynaud-Spanke as the standard reference work on the Old French lyric.[18] Linker adopted the Pillet-Carstens system for Provençal lyric, listing first the poets in alphabetical order with their poems in alphabetical order by the first word of the first line. Linker numbers are thus in two parts: 1-1 indicating poet and poem. In his review in *Speculum*, January 1981, Nathaniel Smith recommends the use of Pillet-Carsten's system of a separating period (1.1) in order to facilitate sequential listings (1.1-5). The Linker *Bibliography* includes a concordance so that the Raynaud numbers may be easily converted into the new Linker numbers. In the present work I will designate both Raynaud and Linker numbers for Old French lyrics. Thus the *chanson de toile* "La belle Doe siet au vent" would be R744/265.963 (adopting N. Smith's use of the separating period). The Linker number 265 is the category 'anonymous'--a large group of 1751 lyrics. Linker includes motets and rondeaux in his classification; genres that were excluded by Raynaud for the most part. Valuable features of the text include musical information, a list of Provençal manuscripts containing French lyrics, an index of twenty-two longer works containing French lyrics, and a list of French versions of Provençal poems.

Italian lyric before 1300 is traditionally divided for critical purposes into three schools: 1) the Sicilian, 2) the transitional, or "Siculo-Toscano" school, and 3) the *stilnovisti* school. The Sicilian school flourished at the court of Frederick II during the period of his reign, 1220-1250. The poets were amateurs, not professional jongleurs or troubadours, but notaries, advocates, administrators, and functionaries in Frederick's government. Since their poetic production extends over a period of thirty years, some critics attempt to show a "two-generation" division in the development of styles, but the weight of critical opinion maintains that this poetry was essentially static in form and content, borrowing consistently from Provençal models. Typical genres used by the poets were the *canzoni*, *sirventesi*, *discordi*, and *sonetti*, with an occasional *ballata*. The corpus is characterized by rigid adherence to conventional modes, and to a vocabulary of business and legal terms.

The definitive edition of Sicilian lyric poetry is *Le Rime della Scuola Siciliana*, by Bruno Panvini.[19] Three hundred and twenty lyrics are arranged by attribution in three sections: 1) by named author, 2) by doubtful attribution, and 3) anonymous. Significantly, while the sections of named authors and doubtful attributions contain nearly equal numbers (42 and 30) the anonymous category is by far the largest portion, with one hundred and thirty-six poems. Sixteen songs, or five per cent of the total, have direct female speech. Nine of the sixteen come from the anonymous section. Of the remainder, Giacomo da Lentino, the leading figure of the school and perhaps the earliest sonnet writer, uses no female speech, but Frederick uses a female *persona* for one poem, "Dolze meo drudo, eh, vatène," and M. Rinaldo D'Aquino uses it for two lyrics. Likewise, other poets have only one or two women's voice lyrics in their extant repertoires. In this edition Panvini provides a stemma that looks like a floor plan for a Vitruvian palazzo showing the placing of the two dozen or so manuscripts for this corpus that date as early as 1288. He writes that discrepancies in attribution are traceable back to the earliest manuscripts. It happened frequently that the same song would be given five times to one poet, and five times to another. Or five different attributions for one song would be assigned. He lists the most obvious discrepancies from the earliest manuscripts.

Transitional and <u>stilnovisti</u> poets may be studied in the Ricciardi edition of <u>La Litteratura Italiana</u>, Volume Two, edited by Gianfranco Contini and titled <u>Poeti del Duecento</u> (in two volumes).[20] This 1960 publication has abundant notes for the poems along with biographical and bibliographical information for each poet. Older sources that should also be consulted are Carducci, <u>Antica Lirica Italiana</u> and the <u>Crestomazia Italiana dei Primi Secoli</u>, whose first 19th-century editor was Ernesto Monaci, editor of the Vatican manuscript of Galician-Portuguese lyric.[21] Alfredo Schiaffini, editor of the 1955 revision, relates in his preface some of the history of scholarship that resulted in our possession of medieval Italian texts.

Dramatic monologues and <u>tenzone</u> with a female voice may be found in texts of the "Tuscan realist" school or the "Scuola Guittoniana." They are written by Guittone D'Arezzo, Bondie Dietaiuti di Firenze, Rustico Filippi, and Cecco Angiolieri. Although these poets also wrote love sonnets, they are known primarily for their satirical and comic songs. A few songs with female speech are found inserted in the margins or blank spaces of government documents of the thirteenth century. Thus the <u>Memoriali Bolognesi</u> of 1282 is the source for a half-dozen songs of a vulgar nature: drinking songs, a dialogue of two townswomen discussing their husbands, a young woman pleading with her grandfather to find a husband for her.

Lyrics of <u>dolce stil novo</u> contain little or no direct female speech. This is true almost by definition, since the "sweet style" in a "new" way, that is, interiorized and intellectualized, dwells on the inner life of the speaking male in speculative contemplation rather than in outwardly projected dramatic situations. The convention of the singing <u>pastora,</u> for instance, is continued in Guido Cavalcanti's "In un boschetto trova' pasturella," but she is <u>reported</u> to be singing ("cantava comme fosse 'namorata") and we hear no direct speech. The use of voices other than the poet's (prosopopeia) becomes abstract: the God of Love, a voice of conscience, and allegorized qualities. Thus Guido

Guinizzelli creates an allegorized figure of Hope, "la Speranza," who comforts the narrator in "Lamentoni di mia disaventura." Female speech written by Dante is a large subject which naturally invites our attention. It relates, I believe, to his use of Provençal speech models. If the *Fiori* are an early creation of Dante, as John Took argues in a recent article, we see there "les pattes du maître futur" in the vulgar songs in direct speech, many of which are in a female *persona*.[22] In the *Vita nuova* the beloved is elevated beyond speech, while lesser ladies comment, question, and sympathize. Beatrice's speech in the *Comedia* is pungent and intellectual; a style that recalls the special flavor of the female voice in Provençal, which is the subject of Chapter Five of this work.[23]

Our modern critical concept of "voice" has developed in a striking and fundamental way since the books of the Bakhtin circle, written in Russia in the late 1920's, began to circulate in the West in French and English translations.[24] Mikhail Bakhtin, with his associates Medvedev and Voloshinov, challenges stylisticians to look at language and literature as inherently ("atomistically") dialogical. A literary work is not, according to this view, a unified consciousness addressing a uniform receptor, but a resonant, multiform response to diverse stimuli. All language ("langue") and all speech ("parole"), Bakhtin claims, are response. The analysis of a literary work or language should therefore describe this responsiveness and give attention to the "other" voice that is hidden to a greater or lesser degree in every speech, and to the interrelatedness of the various "words" or utterances to be found in every work. His own analyses of Dostoevsky and Rabelais, as well as his critical insights in *The Formal Method in Literature* and *Marxism and the Philosophy of Language*, provide a contemporary theoretical background for the problem of voice, a background within which our ideas of the use and function of the female voice in medieval Romance lyric may be situated. In the following passage from *Problems of Dostoevsky's Poetics*, Bakhtin expresses his orientation toward language:

> The word is not a thing, but rather the eternally mobile, eternally changing medium of dialogical intercourse. It never coincides with a single consciousness or a single voice. The life of the word is in its transferral from one mouth to another, one context to another. In the process the word does not forget where it has been and can never wholly free itself from the dominion of the contexts of which it has been a part.[25]

The conception of language as a "medium of dialogical intercourse," which Bakhtin calls "metalinguistics," allows us to see the female voice as one strand in the medium of words that makes the history of lyric poetry.

The roots of the problem of voice, or the identity and context of the speaker, is in the Platonic separation of <u>diegesis</u>, the speaker speaking for himself, from <u>mimesis</u>, the speaker speaking through an assumed character or <u>persona</u>. A third, or "mixed" style of speech combines the two voices. In this mode, a narrator in a "straight" voice introduces (or may be interrupted by) a voice or voices of assumed or borrowed speech. The second, dependent voice bears the character of quoted or "other" speech, i.e., of a voice taken from its original surroundings to be brought into a new, dialectical relationship with the dominant voice. Modern critics have noted that the third, or "mixed speech" style has been greatly expanded by post-Enlightenment writers, in particular by Robert Browning and Fyodor Dostoevsky, both influential stylists. Writers, following modernist trends in other arts, discarded frames and explanations to expose thought directly as the generative principle of speech. Freed from conventions that strictly separated poetry, drama, and prose, both prose writers (James, Woolf, Joyce) and poets (Hardy, Eliot, Frost, Stevens) entered the mind of a <u>persona</u> to show the movement of thought from multiple perspectives. Fiction and lyric moved toward the mimetic, or dramatic, pole of voice. Thus contemporary criticism necessarily gives a large place to discourse analysis, "inner speech" and intertextuality, the response of one text to another.

When we consider the <u>chansons de femme</u> of medieval Romance lyric from this linguistic and rhetorical point of view, we are dealing clearly with reported/represented speech, a "message within a message." In his review article for <u>PTL</u> in 1978 on free indirect discourse, Brian McHale suggests a loosening of the three categories of traditional speech distinctions to accommodate marginal categories of indirect discourse.[26] We should, he remarks, plot the inclusion of reported speech along a continuum from purely factual to highly "colored." While medieval lyric style separates reported speech from the reporting context quite rigorously, especially when compared to some modern styles, the degree of speech style change varies greatly from language to language and from form to form. Recent work on free indirect discourse reviewed by McHale raises questions which need investigation in regard to medieval lyric: for example, the indices and markers by which the poet signals the approach of reported speech. In this brief discussion of voice theory and the place of the female voice within it, however, we will take up some ideas of Bakhtin and his circle, and find their application in the specific case of the dramatic monologue, a frequent vehicle for the female voice.

In his brilliant discussion of the relation of carnival spirit and literature, Mikhail Bakhtin states that evidence of carnivalistic behavior and its expression in literature is especially manifest at times of social unrest and change. In such periods the age itself is "polyphonic" and the representation of the spirit of carnival gives a powerful symbolic form for comprehending life. Laughter becomes a pervasive and saving element whereby the intensity of public events could be toned down. Catastrophe and scandal take their place in literature as oxymoronic situations. When the sacred and the profane are intensely lived by the whole population, the juxtaposition of the serious and the comic is an everyday experience. No attempt is made at a solution of the problem, no rational causality is present in the carnival spirit; only the temporary relief of pressure is sought in the upwelling of youthful merrymaking.

Mediterranean cultures from very early times have permitted short periods of release from the constraints of hierarchy in the social order. Slaves were freed to dress up as their masters, to dance and play in public, assuming temporarily roles that were denied to them in everyday conduct of life. The reversal of roles helped to alleviate the oppression they customarily experienced and helped to stabilize and support the <u>status quo</u>. The Roman <u>Saturnalia</u> continued the ancient practice of a brief suspension of the normal fear and awe that controlled behavior in unequal power relationships. In medieval centuries the "Boy Bishop" and the "Feast of Fools" and other ceremonial overturnings of religious and civic order served the same function for lower orders of society. At the time of carnival, or during the invocation of the carnival spirit, authority could be mocked, complaints freely spoken, and spontaneous behavior go unpunished. In the area of sexual repression, open eroticism was the spirit of carnival. Sexual pleasure at the scene of religious ceremonies ventilated the "other" side of civilized life; the love of disorder, disruption, chaos.

The female voice, within the overwhelmingly male-dominated literary tradition in written form, can function as a carrier of undercurrents of social values not generally permitted or approved. In the role of a complementary voice, the female voice in reported speech permits a psychic plenitude, a wholeness of emotional expression very valuable to lyric poetry and to its audience. Thus it would <u>not be a foreign element to the male psyche</u>, but a carrier of repressed values, the negative, often childish and archaic, unruly, "anti-establishment" currents that co-exist, as we very well know, in uneasy tension with our positive and rational attitudes which have the assent of <u>most</u> of our <u>librum arbitrium</u>. In its role as the complement to the masculine-identified dominant side of the social psyche, the female voice can carry the projected fears and anxieties of social and economic degradation, religious heterodoxy as well as rebelliousness toward governmental and social oppressions, particularly those associated with the social institution of marriage.

In its capacity as a carrier of "otherness" the female voice participates in what Bakhtin describes so vividly as "carnivalization." As a legitimized comic character, the female speaker in medieval Romance lyric, like her modern sister Eliza Doolittle, permits the latent side of human nature to be revealed and developed in concretely sensuous form. In her moment on the stage of public performance, she can express the bitterness of economic privation and of social ostracism, even (perhaps essentially) linguistic defects with a comic force that wins the sympathy of the audience. Fears and oppositions that must ordinarily be repressed can dress up in the rough cloak of a peasant or poor urban girl, while the female _persona_ and assumed female speech afford protection to the male poet. Officially unpopular ideas and thoughts take the shape of a speaker whose low status limits the liability of the poet.[27]

It is important to recognize the poetic effects made possible by "borrowing" speech. "Quoted" or assumed speech serves different functions in its original and in its secondary contexts. In its original context, it serves the intention of its original owner or owners, so to speak. It is simple and "straight" speech, not double voiced. In the secondary context, it is permeated by another intention, that of the borrowing owner. It is "put to work" in a skewed relation to its new context, often that of irony, parody, polemic, or "coat-tailing." The new owner can be hostile, or partly hostile to the borrowed speech, or there can be an ambiguous love-hate relation to the new speech. Since the consciousness that borrows speech is a multi-voiced one, tension between the voices is inevitable. In his study of Italian dialects, Leo Spitzer writes:

> When we reproduce in our speech a small chunk of our interlocutor's utterance, already by virtue of the change of speakers a change in tone inevitably occurs: on our lips the "other's" words always sound foreign to us, and very often have an intonation of ridicule, exaggeration, or mockery . . . .[28]

"Division is tension" is an axiom of religious and semantic wisdom; Dante's hell is complex, while heaven is a seamless circle, as so many commentators have observed. The interlacing of female speech within medieval Romance lyric, then, provides rich opportunities for poetic effects of parody, satire, hyperbole, and pathos, as well as the thematic force of social release that has been described as carnivalization. A closer look at how the female voice produces the effects of the "skewed" relationship to its male host voice can be obtained if we study the dynamics of the dramatic monologue, the form of many female voice lyrics.

The relation of poet/persona/audience in the performance or reading of a dramatic monologue differs from that of the dramatist/actors/audience in a theatrical performance.[29]
A dramatic monologue is not simply a dramatic soliloquy subtracted from a play. The speaker of a dramatic soliloquy addresses himself, debates issues with himself and takes a decision or resolves a question by the final lines of the speech. The soliloquy advances the plot by creating a new balance of power within the speaker which signals a new possibility of action in the outer world. The one-to-one discussion, when it is completed, is returned to the frame of the plot. In the dramatic lyric, on the other hand, the speaking character is not self-aware; he or she addresses the communication outward; it spills from the character in spite of himself like a spontaneous overflow of emotion. Resolution of the conflict is no part of the speaker's purpose, nor is the achievement of a new inner balance of power. Rather, the poet shares or reveals a single perspective on experience—the lyric moment—by showing (mimesis) the experience at the instant of its happening in virtual time and space. Other characters, objects, and actions are only shadows—hints the poet gives at a minimum in order to focus on the speaker. All the compression of the lyric form is operative.

Another difference between the soliloquy and the dramatic lyric is that the voice of the dramatist is co-terminus with his play. The audience understands by the final words what the play has been about, one hopes. But the voice of the poet in the dramatic monologue must be located beyond the final words of the text—it is at a distance from the surface of the text. In fact, the poet and <u>persona</u> must be in a <u>carefully contrived disequilibrium</u> for the poem to be successful. To achieve a distance from his character, the poet uses extraordinary speakers and situations to accentuate the divorce between poet and <u>persona</u>. By adopting an implausible mask, the poet circumvents the rhetoric of direct statement (the way of diegesis) which invites a rational response of assent or disagreement. Through the use of the problematical mask, the poet no longer addresses our reason, and we do not respond with rational judgment. Rather, he appeals directly to the emotions—using the rhetorical appeal of pathos-to which we must respond, if we respond at all, with empathy. It is only at the conclusion of the experience of the poem that we bring our rational judgement into play, because we become aware that the argument of the poem lies somewhere outside the surface of the text.

Thus, the communication pattern of the dramatic monologue is circular: 1) the poet projects a speaking voice, a _persona_, 2) the listener or reader must enter the poetic experience with that _persona_, and 3) the listener or reader must return to the poet beyond the last word of the lyric to find the whole meaning OF WHICH ONLY A PARTIAL MEANING IS GIVEN BY THE SPEAKER. Often the speakers are obsessed with a single, narrow and passionate point of view, and our sense of reality corrects the distortion. It is in this movement of _correction_ that we comprehend the lyric. We cannot confine our response to a rational consideration of the propositional content of the lyric while we are invited to share a moment of passionate self-revelation. Indeed, the poet relies on the response of our human sympathy. Then, when we have given our assent by sympathy, we experience by judgement the full import of the poem's meaning, i.e. we must go through and beyond the experience of the text.

The more distant the speaker from our experience, the more emphatic will be our imaginative leap of empathy. Thus, wrong or heterodox ideas are more likely to be presented than correct and socially approved ones--ideas are like characters. The possibility of misreading the poet's intention in a dramatic monologue, or of finding various interpretations is always present. The distance between poet and _persona_ problematizes the act of interpretation. In this sense, the dramatic monologue may be likened to a scientific experiment which only approximates or tests the truth of a hypothesis. It presents for our empathetic participation a range of roles and attitudes for us to sample. If we like it we can keep it, if not, we can learn from the virtual experience what we do not want to do or be. The dramatic ambiguity matches the often intellectually ambiguous climate in which this form thrives. The incompleteness deliberately formed by the poem calls for a conclusion to be supplied by the audience. As Langbaum writes:

> The truth of the dramatic lyric is not a propositional truth to which we assent by reason but an experiential truth to which we assent by empathy and intuition. It is not a thing perceived, but a quality of perception.[30]

We must, then, reach the truth of the poem by pragmatically placing ourselves both within and without the speaker's view.

Dramatic monologues in the female voice are found in ancient, medieval, and modern lyric poetry. The possibility of a convention for the literary presentation of the female voice in lyric poetry is suggested by its historical continuity in Western literature. To place the medieval period within a time frame that extends from early Greek lyric to the present century, we will examine in detail two dramatic monologues, one from the Hellenistic period, written by Theocritus, and the other from the thirteenth century, written by Cerverí de Girona. Both lyrics use the voice of a female magician. They illustrate the "carnival" values available to the poet in the female voice; with comic hyperbole he can comment on respected but no longer dominant literary tradition, the tragi-comedy of young love (Theocritus) and the oppressions of unloving unions (Cerverí de Girona). Customarily censored themes are ventilated in speech by means of the implausible mask, the sorceress. We will also look at the female voice as it is used by four modern poets, Thomas Hardy, W.B. Yeats, D.H. Lawrence, and Robert Frost. The excursus on the modern poets will be brief, but will suggest that we are dealing with a living and still influential part of our culture.

Idyll II of Theocritus and "Al fals gelos don Deus mala ventura" of Cerverí de Girona are two lyrics which use the theme of the female magician, or witch, whose supernatural powers create a poetic texture both terrifying and comic. Caught in a moment of intense emotional crisis, she confesses her violently negative feelings toward a man. In spite of the differences of historical period, cultural determinants and authorial skills, the poems, placed side by side, will illustrate some of the characteristic features of the female voice in dramatic lyric.

Theocritus' Second Idyll is one of three "urban mimes" whose settings and cast of characters recall Greek new comedy.[31] It shows the extremely conscious craftsmanship typical of the Alexandrian poets, whose lyrics contain allusions to the poetry of Homer, Sappho, and the great dramatists. Theocritus left his native Syracuse to become a court poet at Alexandria. His sophisticated audience knew its literary heritage, but could not recreate its original splendors; an age of allusion.

The young witch Simaetha speaks a passionate monologue whose contrasting elements build an ironic female voice. The surface texture is grandiose, but it is spoken by a character who cannot live up to the pretensions of the language she appropriates. Stung with pain at the absence of her beloved Delphis, the young sorceress calls on the power of magic to bring him back to her or to send him to hell:

> . . . but now I will bind him with fire-spells. Nay, shine bright O Moon, for to thee, goddess, will I softly chant, and to Hecate of the world below, before whom even the dogs stand shivering, as she comes over the graves of the dead and the dark blood. Hail, grim Hecate, and to the end attend me, and make these drugs of mine as potent as those of Circe or Medea or golden-haired Perimede.[32]

Simaetha's voice is comic in that she is not the Thessalian sorceress Medea of Pindar and Euripides, who could kill men, women and children with her magic, but the girl down the street who cannot keep track of her bay leaves. She attempts the speech of a large and passionate woman, but in reality is more at home talking about the neighbor who has died, or the mother of the flute-player, and her girlfriend Clearista whose cloak she borrowed for the festival:

> And Theumaridas' Thracian nurse, now dead and gone, that dwelt at my door, had begged and besought me to come and see the show. And I, unhappy wretch, went with her, wearing a fair long linen dress, and Clearista' fine wrap over it.

Simaetha lives alone in the city with one slave, Thestylis, with whom she is on friendly terms. She is a bourgeoise, perhaps an orphan, who knows and lives comfortably with her neighbors. She comes from a lower economic class than her lover, Delphis, who is something of a dandy, a frequenter of palaestra and gymnasium. The number of local city characters is surprisingly high, recalling the urban mime of the Syracusan women going to the temple, Idyll XV. Simaetha marks the spot where she first saw Delphis by the name of the person whose house was nearby, Lycon. Placing the trappings of the great women, Medea and Circe, in the hands of a young woman of the city, a character out of the New Comedy or mime, neutralizes the danger of those awesome figures, and by a reductive contrast, gives the audience light amusement rather than serious challenge.

The poem of 166 lines is divided into three parts: the incantation, the recollection of the love affair, and a brief farewell. After calling for her misplaced bay leaves, Simaetha sets forth her grievance against Delphis:

> For eleven days now he has not even visited me. the wretch, and knows not so much as whether I am dead or alive. Nay, he has not once knocked at my door, so cruel is he.

She will go to his wrestling school the next day to scold him. The incantation, one of the most finished passages in Theocritus, consists of nine quatrains separated by a refrain, "Mark, Lady Moon, whence came my love," a command sung to the turn of the iynx wheel. She burns barley, bay leaves and bran. At the third invocation, Hecate herself arrives at the crossroads, and dogs howl in a dreamlike landscape. Simaetha clashes bronze cymbals for protection.

Again the scene is comic because august mysteries are done in haste with an air of theatrical improvisation, as the maid assists:

> Now will I burn the bran. And thou, Artemis, hast power to move Hell's adamant and aught else as stubborn--Thestylis, the dogs are howling in the town; the goddess is at the crossroads. Quick, clash the bronze.

Libations are poured, and a fringe of cloth from a coat Delphis had left at the house is shredded and put into the fire. Thestylis carries herbs to rub on the threshold of Delphis' house, as Simaetha talks of a lizard potion she will take to him. Alone, Simaetha, who now seems like an ordinary young girl, laments her seduction with a full awareness of the loss to her from the affair:

> Lo, still is the sea, the breezes still; yet not still the torment in my breast, but all on fire am I for him that has made me, alas, no wife but a wretched thing, no maiden now.

As she relates the details of the fateful meeting with Delphis, Simaetha shows enthusiasm and curiosity. Many beasts were paraded in honor of Artemis, "among them a lioness." She dresses in her best to see the show, and is overcome by the sight of the beautiful Delphis walking with his friend. She dramatizes her lovesick condition in the following days, and sends the maid to bring Delphis to her:

> And oftimes my color would turn as pale as fustic, and all my hair was falling from my head, and bones alone were left of me, and skin. And to whose house did I not go, what hag's did I pass over, of those that had skill in charms?

Delphis arrives with words as sweet as his appearance. He delivers a speech full of elegant self-praise, and the gullible Simaetha is overcome, "ever too easy won."

> And, with a glance at me, the lover untrue fixed his eyes upon the ground, and sat down upon the couch, and sitting, spoke: "Truly, Simaetha, with thy summons to this house thou didst outrun my coming by no more than I of late outran the charming Philinus."

The poem ends swiftly in a manner that marks Simaetha's petty bourgeoise class status. She hears from a neighborhood gossip that Delphis is in love with another. The mixture of phrases of classical epic with her neighborhood gossip keeps the tone comic:

> But to-day, when the steeds of rosy Dawn were bearing her swiftly up the sky from Ocean, there came to me the mother of Philista, our flute-player, and of Melixo; and many another thing she told me, and how that Delphis was in love.

Finding comfort in the activity of her fantasy, Simaetha vows to send Delphis to hell. As she bids farewell to the moon, she promises to bear her pain bravely:

> But do thou farewell, Lady, and turn thy steeds towards the Ocean. And I will bear my longing as till now I have endured it. Moon on thy gleaming throne, farewell, and farewell ye other stars that follow the car of quiet Night.

If we reconstruct the changing role of Delphis in the poem and place that movement against the moods of Simaetha, we understand the delights of this poem for its audience. Our first view of Delphis is that of a cruel rake, able to inflict pain on the woman he has abandoned. Delphis is associated in the incantation to Theseus for unfaithfulness and to Bacchus for ardor. In the nostalgic recreation of the opening and happy days of the romance, Delphis is a shining youth, irresistably persuasive, an athlete loved by his friends, a faultless lover. He joins Simaetha in a mood of harmony. In the third part of the poem Delphis is again threatened with punishment if he abandons Simaetha; a danger removed immediately by her subsequent calm resignation. A reading of the poem from this point of view shows that the listener who identifies with Delphis would move from a <u>frisson</u> of pleasure at being called cruel and heartless by a passionate woman forced to employ dark arts to keep him, to an enjoyable retelling of a conquest, to the assurance of impunity following a touch of the earlier danger. The woman is delightfully and impotently mad, but she will accept her loss. Elitist males of the audience identifying with Delphis would have "had without being had," as a vulgar Greek expression put the power relationship of higher to lower caste. Simaetha is mocked as a lower caste bourgeoise in her social milieu of working girls and servants, her ludicrous attempts at grand language (which nevertheless flatters the audience) and her desperate attempt to recover a loss that is irreparable to her and of no importance to others.

Theocritus shows in other poems that he is a close analyst of the potential for pain in male-female relationships. Idyll Six, spoken in equal parts by Damoetas and Daphnis, concerns the teasing of Polyphemus by Galatea. Daphnis calls her a deliberately cruel wanton. Damoetas reveals that he is using her own methods on her, keeping her passion hot only until he has her consent to marry. Idyll Twenty, spoken by Eunica and a herdsman, has a city lady refusing the countryman in seven lines of fierce invective, while the rest of the powm is filled with his lament. In Idyll Eight, Daphnis describes his manner towards a young "dark-brown" girl who loves him. He deliberately will not look at her, but keeps his eyes on the floor; this is the eye movement Simaetha reports about Delphis.

The woman who turns to witchcraft because of a disappointment in love is the subject of a monologue by the Provençal poet Cerverí de Girona. Shorter and less exquisitely fashioned than the Greek poem, the medieval work has the same tone of eager determination to change fate by means of a spell. Perhaps Cerverí had Idyll II in mind, although the sorceress theme would be available to him in Virgil, Eclogue VIII, and Horace, Epode V, or simply in his own surrounding world.

Cerverí de Girona, the pseudonym of Guilhem de Cervera, is a late Provençal poet (1250-1280) whose extant corpus, the largest of any troubadour, consists of one hundred and nineteen poems.[33] T.G. Bergin calls him

> a stylist of remarkable virtuosity. His cultivation of popular forms is interesting: he offers _dansas_, _baladas_, _estampidas_, and _espingaduras_ as well as _pastorelas_. At the other extreme, in his hands, the _trobar ric_ goes out with no mere whimper . . .[34]

The first eight poems of the Riquer edition are in a popular style; among them is the well-known _viandela_ (road song) "Jana delgada." Cerverí has caught a conversational, low comedy tone in his lyric "Al fals gelos don Deus mala ventura" that Martín de Riquer calls "interesantísima por sus alusiones a la brujería . . .[35]

> Al fals gelos don Deus mala ventura
> car lo solaz me tol de mon amich,
> e·m da mal pus lo pris, car tan me dura.
>
> Pero d'aytan me tenc per be segura
> que no viura catre jorns, aça·us dic,
> que·l pausaray sus el pols tal untxura
> que·l auzira, lo fals gelos enich.
> E a'm fatxa una bon'escriptura
> mos amis douz, que sus el col li lic,
> e ma mayre, que tot jorn lo conjura.
>
> Sabetz que·m fa'l gelos laia figura
> can s'es colgatz, sol del dir ay fastich:
> l'esquenaça·m gira, c'a negr'e dura,
> e pus aspra que fuylla de jaric,

e puys rimfla e polsa ses mesura.
Si•n breu de tems de negre me'n abric,
car anc no vi pus fera criatura!

Luyn es de gaug, pres d'ir'e de rancura
qui marit a fexuch, fals ne enich,
qu'eu o say be, per ma desventura,
c'un veyll ruat me deren mey amic,
c'ab sa suor me malmet e•m madura;
quil ve, sis vol tardar de mal destrich,
diga'l que Deus li do bona pastura.

La domn'als Cartz e Sobrepretz atura
valor ab si, e•l Enfans a cor ric
de mantener pretz e patz e dretura.

Martín de Riquer has made a Spanish translation, but I will give the English of Kurt Lewent:

1. To the false jealous man may God give bad luck for he deprives me of the company of my friend and has caused me trouble since I took him. Why does he live so long?

2. But I think I can be quite sure that he will not live four days longer, I tell you. For I shall put on his temple such an unguent as will kill him, the false jealous scoundrel. And my sweet friend has written for me an efficient spell which I shall fasten to his neck, and my mother casts spells over him every day.

3. You must know that the jealous man. when he has lain down to sleep, offers to me [such] an unpleasant aspect [that] I feel disgusted only by speaking of it: he turns his backbone towards me, which is black and hard and rougher than oak leaves, and then he breathes hard and snores beyond measure. [I wonder] whether I shall really free myself in a short time of that abominable man. For never did I see a fiercer creature.

4. Far from joy and near to sorrow and grief is the one who has an annoying, false and malicious husband, and I know it only too well by my own misfortune; for my friends gave me an old wrinkled man, who with his sweat makes me sick and nauseates me. If a person meets

>   him, and wants to protect himself from injury, let him express the wish that God will give him good pasture.
>
> 5. The Lady of the Thistles and "Extra Fine" keep worth with them, and the Infante shows a noble endeavor to maintain courtliness and peace and justice.[36]

This sorceress is cast in the role of the medieval malmariée. Together with her mother and lover, she plots the death of her "fals gelos." She gloats happily over the prospect of his demise, which should take place in four days. One can easily imagine the potential for comic oral presentation in these lines. She is active, like Simaetha, and confident that her alliance with the power of nature forms a combination stronger than the oppressive marriage that frustrates her. Her magic is an unguent that she has put on "el pols," and a sentence of words, written by her lover and placed under her husband's pillow. The mother's contribution is to chant the sentence all day. Again we see the woman surrounded by members of her social group, who form her supporters in her project, just as Simaetha is shown with her maid and neighbors who give assistance and take part in the drama.

The opening tercet acts as a refrain in this dança lyric, presumably sung by the chorus while the three stanzas were sung by a soloist. The two other chansons de malmariée in Provençal are both anonymous, "Coindeta sui, si com n'ai greu cossire" and "Quan lo gilos er fora." Other songs mention the "gilos" but without the specific tone of complaint that we find in these three lyrics. The manuscript Sa (Biblioteca de Catalunya, Number 146) in Barcelona is unusual in not being an anthology but devoted entirely to Cerverí, making him one of the few troubadours of whom we have, presumably, a complete repertoire. The manuscript designates this poem a gelosesca, a word derived from gelos and formed after the model of the word sirventesca, originally the feminine of an adjective in esc. No other songs of Cerverí bear this title, but the stanza form 10a' 10b 10a' 10b 10a' 10b 10' is exactly that of one earlier song, by Montan, a contemporary of Sordello, with whom he exchanged a cobla. Montan's poem, writes Kurt Lewent, is an incredibly obscene travesty of courtly love. It was accepted medieval poetic practice to model satirical songs on previous compositions, although the canso was supposed to have a unique melody and rhyme pattern. Whether or not Cerverí took his form for the poem from Montan or from a now lost example we cannot know, but the association would place Cerverí's song within the category of humorous or satirical songs. The word esquernaça ("eschine") is a unica, although formed on expressions in Spanish: carnasa, filasa, golasa, and is in the context of other hispanisms. It undoubtedly has a comic, hyperbolic effect. The theme of the husband's "eschine" continues to be found in examples of the malmariée song in later centuries.

In his 1971 study of medieval Spanish satire, Kenneth Scholberg describes the work of Cerverí de Girona, a major Catalan satirist, as "algo triste, pesimista, que en momentos llega a tomar un tono desesperado."[37] In his denunciations of the rich and powerful and his defense of troubadours and jongleurs, Cerverí does not resemble the satirists among the Galician-Portuguese poets who are witty in their burlesques. Rather, "La composición de Cerverí es totalmente seria, exhortando al juglar a una vida mejor." It is as a misogynist that Cerverí was remembered; his long poem "Maldit-Bendit" gives by far the larger part to the defamation of women; the short retraction, or "Bendit" seems almost pro forma. In some parts of this poem Cerverí shows the brilliant wit of the Provençal tradition, but for the most part the wit seems perfunctory, at least to a modern reader.

The witchcraft poems of Theocritus and Cerverí provide two examples of a continuing theme in the woman's voice in Mediterranean literature. Each of the "witches" pits her will against the misery of an unhappy sexual relationship. Her cries are made comic through an ironic context shared by poet and audience. Because she is the speaker, she gains the natural empathy of the audience, but because she is an outcast, an outsider to the ideal state of the audience (no one expects or wants to be unhappy) she is placed at a negative distance where she can be observed and then dismissed. A projected persona, she is both real and unreal; real as an image in the minds of poet and audience, and unreal as an incomplete, indeed, skewed version of the fullness of experience. The repetition of the image, however, through many centuries and political changes, points to the stability of the convention. It is part of the function of a mask to stabilize and reinforce our perception of experience; the female voice persona in dramatic lyric performs that function in the area of perception of sexual role stereotypes.

In our own time, major poets such as Yeats, Hardy, Lawrence, and Frost have drawn on similar resources to adapt the ancient conventions of the female voice to contemporary lyrics.[38] All four poets knew dialects of country people; all four had experience with village life and old tales. All four were well educated in the classical Western heritage of poetry, and they found themes and forms for female voice lyrics that match those from ancient and medieval examples. Hardy knew and copied medieval Latin lyric, and used its meters. Yeats, a founder of the Irish renaissance, loved the Celtic stories and may have derived his portraits of speaking women from the same models that influenced medieval Romance, a story familiar to medievalist scholars. Verse forms of fragmentation and incorporation typical of medieval verse (as we shall see in the following chapter) are present: the frame, debate, pivot, and coda; also refrains, nonsense words, "primary exclamations" and strange speech. Like Theocritus and Cerverí de Girona, Yeats and Frost write in the voice of "witches." Yeats' "Solomon and the Witch" is less elaborate than Frost's "The Witch of Coös," but his "Crazy Jane" sequence shows how powerfully he can use the abnormal female to contrast and complement his own "normal" Zeitgeist. Of the four poets, only Hardy did not write drama; since the 1960 performances in Nottingham and London of Lawrence's plays and the publication of criticism on this area of his work, we cannot think of him only as a poet and novelist. The dramatic imagination, a powerful drive in the poetic creativity of all of these writers, led to remarkably congruent settings for their female characters.

    The convention of the poor, downtrodden or lamenting female "outsider" is presented with particular force by Yeats and Hardy. Yeats' first group of ballads (from Crossways, 1889) includes "The Ballad of Moll Magee," a story of a young working mother, who, desperate for sleep, smothers her new baby in her bed. Her husband casts her out, and she finds shelter in a friend's house. The grim words of comfort the friend speaks are to wait a while, the husband will come and fetch her home again. Hardy's "To an Unborn Pauper Child" shows a mother hoping her child will not live, and thus escape the pains and fears of the harsh world. Both poets use the voice of dead women longing to be a part of life. Yeats' "Three Things" shows a dead woman, symbolized by a bone on a shore, telling of the three things she knows; baby, husband, and sex. Hardy, who frequently uses the voice of a dead woman, wrote in "Her Immortality" of a woman speaking from her coffin to her lover who attends her graveside. She implores him not to join her in death so she can come to the upper world when he calls, as he is the only one who calls for her. "In Childbed" (Hardy) shows a grandmother appearing to her daughter who is in bed nursing a new baby. The grandmother cautions that the present hope and ecstasy will turn to "other views . . . by and by." Both Yeats and Hardy use the voice of Mary, mother of Jesus. Yeats' "The Mother of God" shows Mary in awe of her son, with the contemporary speech . . . "Or strikes a sudden chill into my bones/ And bids my hair stand up?" Hardy's poem has an ironic Mary disgruntled and unnerved by her son's behavior: "Would he'd not mix with the lowest folk--like those fishermen--." His "An Evening in Galilee" clearly has Mary make an unholy suggestion about Jesus' parentage, "That no one knows but Joseph and - one other."

Women at work on the farm and in the kitchen are seen in lyrics of Yeats, Hardy, and Frost. Yeats' "Song of the Old Mother" recalls the famous lines of Virgil about the good wife who rises before dawn to start rhe household work:

> I rise in the dawn, and I kneel and blow
> Till the seed of the fire flicker and glow;
> And then I must scrub and bake and sweep
> Till stars are beginning to blink and peep.

She is aware that the young people still in their beds have no thoughts of her labor, but are dreaming of ribbons and dances. The wife of Hardy's "The Pine Planters" speaks an inner monologue, whose plain speech and level communication may be a forerunner of Frost's great monologues of hill women:

> We work here together
>   In blast and breeze
> He fills the earth in
>   I hold the trees.
>
> He does not notice
>   That what I do
> Keeps me from moving
>   And chills me through.

Hardy, who was a fiddler and knew country dances and music from childhood, uses rhyme and regular meters in a way Frost does not, but the empathy with the female onlooker, who can only verbalize her observations to herself, is similar in both poets.

Women in love is a dominant theme. Lawrence's mother-daughter dialogue in the early lyric, "Whether or Not" is a magnificent example of the type of lyric of which we have many medieval examples in Old French and Galician-Portuguese. The women speak in the Lancashire dialect of Lawrence's childhood experience. To English ears, it signifies country people, and archaic, rough manners. The daughter has heard that her intended husband has made an older woman pregnant. She is shocked, and asks her mother's help. The mother, realist, disillusions her daughter:

> Tha doesna mean ter say ter me, mother,
>   He's gone wi' that--
> --My gel, owt'll do for a man i' th' dark;
>   Tha's got it flat!
> But 'er's old, mother, 'er's twenty year
>   Older nor him--
> --Ay, an' yaller as a crowflower; an' yet i' th' dark
>   Er'd do for Tim.

The poem's strophic form, repetitions and dialectal speech make it an example of the tradition of women's voice lyric. The themes concern men as much as women. In the above lyric, for example, the women are reacting to Tim's action. In Hardy's "Her Reproach" a neglected wife speaks sarcastically about the mediocre work her husband loves; it is her only rival. In "His Heart" (Hardy) a newly bereaved wife assesses her husband's good qualities with a detached and cold reasonableness. In the conflict of young lover and married woman, the poets have a theme on which to invent variations. The material of a <u>malmariée</u> provides the drama of Hardy's "A Conversation at Dawn." A new wife confesses that her beloved has just returned from far away, and he hopes to marry her now because his wife is dead. The new husband will not let her go, but will punish her all her life for her "foolishness." Robert Frost's "The Witch of Coös" seems almost a continuation of that story forward in time. There the old woman tells a passing stranger (the narrator) of her dutifulness through the years to a husband who murdered her lover. The lover is present in her "cracked" mind as a skeleton who mounts the stairs from his grave in the cellar to be locked in the attic, from where he knocks on her bedroom door. She tries to find a finger bone of the skeleton in her button box, and plays on the children's rhyme "Button, button, who's got the button." Frost's tone of playful hallucination, contained sexual hysteria and need for confession creates a portrait of a mind that pays a terrible price for the years of repressed desire.[39]

"Crazy Jane" of Yeats' 1931 <u>Words for Music Perhaps</u> was modeled, according to a letter from Yeats to Olivia Shakespear "upon an old woman who lives in a little cottage near Gort . . . and has an amazing power of audacious speech. . . . She is the local satirist and a really terrible one."[40] In his concern for the relations of body and spirit, Yeats uses the mask of Crazy Jane to express the commitment he feels at this time to the life of the body. A Theosophist and believer in metaphysics, he had to make a special effort to affirm the right place of physical existence, and he does this through a female voice, although her representation of earthly sensuality has nuances requiring careful analysis of the poem sequence. The seven "Crazy Jane" songs of experience are balanced by seven songs of innocence in the "girl and lover" sequence. Two poems of "normal" love follow the two extreme positions: "Three Things," which we mentioned above, and "Lullaby" a lyric that gives a womanly sense of comfort in spite of "all the world's alarms."[41] It is significant that at the time Yeats was expressing a new equilibrium in the struggle of spirit and flesh, he used the female voice to mask a part of his new emotional truth. In <u>Songs for Music Perhaps</u> not only Crazy Jane, but also unnamed young girls and experienced mothers and women convey Yeats' renewed appreciation of physical life.

This short excursion into modern lyric poetry and the female voice could be extended to include other poets, both those like Randall Jarrell, whose lyrics are frequently in the female voice, and others who use it hardly at all. We could also look at the question of the effect on male poets of the increased publication of poetry by women poets, with the resulting respect for women's "prise de la parole." Such questions will have to await a study of the female voice in the modern period used as "borrowed" speech. I hope that the few pages devoted to four recent poets will show how vital is the convention of the female voice in lyric poetry.

Notes to Chapter 1

[1] Jeanroy, "Elles nous transportent dans un monde irréal, d'où est bannie toute contrainte . . . " Alfred Jeanroy, Histoire sommaire de la poésie Occitane (Paris: Didier, 1945), p. 77.

[2] Cynthia P. Bagley, "Cantigas de amigo and cantigas de amor," BHS. 43 (1966), p. 249.

[3] James Monroe and David Swiatlo, "Ninety-Three Arabic Ḫarǧas in Hebrew Muwaśśaḥs: Their Hispano-Romance Prosody and Thematic Features," Journal of the American Oriental Society, 97, No. 2 (1977), 141-63.

[4] Marcelino Menéndez y Pelayo, "De las influencias semíticas en la literatura española," Estudios y discursos de crítica histórica y literaria, ed. by Enrique Sánchez Reyes, I (Santander: CSIC, 1941), pp. 192-217, quotation from p. 218.

[5] Yitzhak F. Baer, [The Political Position of the Jews in Spain in the Time of Judah Halevi] (in Hebrew) Sion, I (1936) 6-23.

[6] Samuel Miklos Stern, "Les Vers finaux en espagnol dans les muwaśśahs hispano-hébraique: une contribution à l'histoire du muwaśśaḥ et à l'étude du vieux dialecte espagnol 'mozarabe,'" Al-Andalus XIII (1948), 229-438. Rep. in English trans. "The Final Lines of Hebrew Muwashshahs from Spain," in Hispano-Arabic Strophic Poetry: Studies by Samuel Miklos Stern, ed. by L.P. Harvey (Oxford: Clarendon, 1974) 123-160.

[7] See Aurelio Roncaglia, "Di una tradizione lirica pretrovadoresca in lingua volgare," Cultura Neolatina XI (1951) 213-49; Leo Spitzer, "The Mozarabic Lyric and Theodor Frings' Theories," Comparative Literature IV (1952), pp. 1-22; Peter Dronke, Medieval Latin and the Rise of European Love Lyric I. Problems and Interpretations (Oxford: Clarendon, 1965), pp. 26-32, 113, 274-7; Theodor Frings, "Altspanische Mädchenlieder aus des Minnesangs Frühling: Anlässlich eines Aufsatzes von Dámaso Alonso," Beiträge zur Geschichte der Deutschen Sprache und Literatur LXXIII (1951), pp. 176-196.

[8] Pierre Groult, "Un siècle de plus pour la poésie espagnole," Les Lettres Romanes V (1951), pp. 39-45.

[9] José María Sola Solé, Corpus de poesía mozárabe; las ḫarǰas andalusíes (Barcelona: Ediciones Hispam, 1973).

10 Carolina Michaëlis de Vasconcellos, Cancioneiro da Ajuda (Halle: 1904, photographic re-edition, Turin: 1966).

11 Henry H. Carter, Cancioneiro da Ajuda (New York: MLA, 1941); Marques Braga, Cancioneiro da Ajuda, Vol. 1, (Lisbon: Livr. Sa de Costa, 1945).

12 Enrico Molteni, Il Canzoniere Portoghese Colocci-Brancuti (Halle: Max Niemeyer, 1880); Elza Paxeco Machado and José Pedro Machado, Cancioneiro da Biblioteca Nacional, Antigo Colocci-Brancuti (Lisbon: Edicio da Revista de Portugal [1949]) 8 vol., in 7 [vol. 7, 1960].

13 Teofilo Braga, Cancioneiro Português da Vaticana (Lisbon: Imp. Nacional, 1878).

14 Jean-Marie D'Heur, Nomenclature des troubadours galiciens-portugais (XIIe-XIVe siècles). Table de concordance de leurs chansonniers, et liste des incipit de leurs compositions (Paris: Arquivos do Centro Cultural Portugues VII, 1973), pp. 17-100.

15 José Joaquim Nunes, Cantigas d'amigo dos trovadores galego-portugueses (Coimbra: Imp. da Universidade, 1926-28) 3 Vol.; Manuel Rodrigues Lapa, Cantigas d'escarnho e de mal dizer, Colección Filolóxica, (n.p.: Ed. Galaxia, 1970).

16 Alfred Pillet and Henry Carstens, Bibliographie der Troubadours, Schriften der Königsberger gelehrten Gesellschaft, Sonderreihe 3 (Halle: 1933, rep. 1968).

17 Hans Spanke, G. Raynauds Bibliographie des altfranzösischen Liedes (Leiden: E.J. Brill, 1955).

18 Robert White Linker, A Bibliography of Old French Lyrics, Romance Monographs, Inc. No. 31, (University, Miss.: Romance Monographs, Inc., 1979).

19 Bruno Panvini, Le Rime della scuola siciliana (Firenze: Olschki, 1962).

20 Gianfranco Contini, Poeti del Duecento, 2 vol., La Letteratura italiana storia e testi, Vol. 2, ed. Ricciardi, (Milano: Ricciardi, 1960).

21 Giosuè Carducci, Antica Lirica Italiana (Firenze: n.p., 1907). Ernesto Monaci, Crestomazia Italiana dei Primi Secoli (Roma: Società Ed. Dante Alighieri, 1955).

22 John Took, "Towards an Interpretation of the Fiori," Speculum LIV, no. 3, (July 1979), 500-528.

23 See Chapter Five, pp. 145-60.

24   Books of the "Bakhtin circle" include: Mikhail Bakhtin, *Problems of Dostoevsky's Poetics,* trans. by R. W. Rotsel, [Ann Arbor, Mich.] Ardis, [1973]; P. N. Medvedev and M. M. Bakhtin, *The Formal Method in Literary Scholarship,* trans. by Albert J. Wehrle, Goucher College Series (Baltimore: Johns Hopkins Univ. Press, 1978); V. N. Volosinov, *Marxism and the Philosophy of Language,* trans. by Ladislav Matejka and I. R. Titunik. Univ. of Chicago Series in Language I, Michael Silverstein, ed., (New York and London: Seminar Press, 1973).

25   Mikhail Bakhtin, *Problems of Dostoevsky's Poetics,* p. 167.

26   Brian McHale, "Free Indirect Discourse: A Survey of Recent Accounts," *PTL: A Journal for Descriptive Poetics and Theory of Literature* 3 (1978), pp. 249-287.

27   I am indebted to Professor Ralph Rader of the University of California, Berkeley, for this phrase, in personal conversation.

28   Leo Spitzer, quoted in Bakhtin, *Problems of Dostoevsky's Poetics,* p. 161.

29   I am indebted to Robert Langbaum for the material on the rhetoric of dramatic monologue. See his *The Poetry of Experience* (New York: Norton, 1957).

30   Langbaum, p. 65.

31   See A. S. F. Gow, *Theocritus: Texts and Commentary,* 2 Vol. (Cambridge: Cambridge Univ. Press, 1950).

32   The translation is that of Gow, *Theocritus,* Vol. 1, *Texts,* p. 17-29.

33   Martín de Riquer, *Obras Completas de Cerverí de Girona* (Barcelona: Instituto Español de Estudios Mediterráneos, 1947).

34   R. T. Hill and T. G. Bergin, *Anthology of the Provençal Troubadours.* 2nd. ed. Rev. by T. G. Bergin, (New Haven: Yale Univ. Press, 1973) Vol. 1, p. 255.

35   Martín de Riquer, *Obras Completas de Cerverí de Girona,* No. 8, p. 17.

36   Kurt Lewent, "An Old Provençal Chanson de Malmariée," *Romanic Review* 37 (1946), 3-19.

37   Kenneth R. Scholberg, *Sátira e invectiva en la España medieval* (Madrid: Gredos [1971]).

[38] I have used the following editions: W. B. Yeats, <u>The Collected Poems</u> (London: Macmillan, 1961); Thomas Hardy, <u>The Collected Poems of Thomas Hardy</u>, ed. James Gibson, (New York: Macmillan, [1976]; Robert Frost, <u>Complete Poems of Robert Frost</u> (New York: Holt, Rinehart and Winston, [1964]); D. H. Lawrence, <u>Collected Poems</u> (New York: Jonathan Cape and Harrison Smith, 1929).

[39] See Frank Lentricchia's discussion of the place of crazy women in Frost's lyric poetry in his <u>Robert Frost: Modern Poetics and the Landscape of Self</u> (Durham, North Carolina: Duke University Press, 1975). "The crazed, the half-crazed, and the about-to-be crazed women that Frost writes about are projections of a self that he fears might have been, a self forced to live, as the wife in "Home Burial," as his deranged sister Jeannie lived, in a room with only one view--that of the graveyard." p. 74.

[40] Quoted in John Unterecker, <u>A reader's guide to William Butler Yeats</u> (New York: Octagon Books, 1971) p. 225.

[41] See Unterecker, p. 230.

Chapter 2

All I want is a room somewhere,
Far away from the cold night air,
With one enormous chair,
Oh, wouldn't that be loverly.

I'm gonna wash that man right outa' my hair,
I'm gonna wash that man right outa' my hair,
I'm gonna wash that man right outa' my hair,
And send him on his way.

Binary (AAAB) rhyme patterns in two 20th century women's songs

THE FEMALE VOICE DETERMINES POETIC FORM

Dialectical analysis of a literary work sees the "other" or subdominant voice as the determiner of form.[1] This is so because it is not called forth, or "placed" according to a prior aesthetic idea, but exists independently in the linguistic environment and is <u>responded to</u> by the dominant, i.e. (in our context) male voice. The creative and aesthetic energy of the poet is used to guide the response in ways appropriate to his culture's needs. Different verse forms in lyric poetry "hear" the message of the "other" (female) voice in different ways and transmit it in various combinations. Accordingly, the female voice in courtly literature appears as fragments in various sectors of the poem where its presence creates various poetic effects. Five such patterns of fragmentation and incorporation of the female voice within the larger male-voice lyric corpus will be discussed and exemplified in this chapter.

Speech that is taken up and used in a second context, as is the case with female speech within medieval Romance lyric, becomes "double-voiced," i.e. it carries an original intention as well as the intention of the new context; often parody, irony, or comedy of lighter or more serious nature. As we noted in Chapter One, only speech that was "unconditioned" or "single-voiced" (i.e. charged with a single intention) in a former context is used to serve a second intention. In an age that is accustomed to frequent use of "double-voiced" speech, unconditioned speech sounds raw, plain, even barbarous. The habit of double-voicing or parodic use of speech can permeate a speech community. An acquired taste, it often signals the presence of a value code, linguistic sophistication, and class differences.

More than a thousand of the extant lyrics in Romance vernacular languages of the medieval period use the female voice, roughly one poem in ten. We can study their forms best in two large groups: 1) the two-part lyrics (what Alfred Jeanroy called les chansons à personnages) and 2) the monologues. The two groups are almost numerically equal, although the two-part lyrics are more widely distributed. Two-voice lyrics with a female voice include all the Mozarabic Spanish ḫarǧas found in the Arabic muwashshahat (described in Chapter 1 and in detail in Section One of this Chapter); all the Old French chansons de toile, the pastorelas, the male-female debates, or tensos and conversos.[2] The majority of the true monologues are found in the Galician-Portuguese corpus, where the female voice is distinguished from the male voice by the use of nature imagery, tone, binary rhymes, and a proliferation of refrain types. Thus, both infra- and inter-lyric structures mark the female voice as different and distinct from the male voice, and as a sub-dominant voice dependent for its existence upon its reporting context.

These complex structures are not confined to male-female speech combinations. The same lyric forms are used for dual presentations of male/male and female/female voice encounters and exchanges. Male voice confrontations are, indeed, the most common style of the debate, or tenso, form, and the male/female debate a much less frequent variation. The two-voice structures provide "slots" in various positions in the lyric and permit the realization of various dramatic tonalities. "Borrowed" or "other" speech enters a dialectical relationship through the song style, and the "other" speech may belong, as we noted in Chapter 1, to animals, angels, or objects of interest to a particular culture. In all formal arrangements which include "borrowed" speech, however, one voice will be dominant and the other subdominant. In no case is female speech independent of its reporting voice in medieval Romance courtly lyric; a reporting voice which is clearly male and dominant.

We can visualize the structures of response of the male voice to female speech by means of Figure 1, which shows visual patterns for five types of male/female voice relationship. I will discuss and compare each of the verse forms briefly, then exemplify each form in a detailed examination of a single lyric. Form I, the CODA, permits the female voice to appear only once in the lyric, in the closing lines, a powerful rhetorical position.[3] From that place the female voice can act as a retrospective comment on the entire portion in the male voice. It can also have the effect of shock and surprise. Although introduced by the dominant male voice, the female speaker slips away from its grasp, so to speak, and addresses the audience or other characters within the mini-scenario of the last few lines. The audience must adduce the parodistic intention of the

Figure 1

THE FRAGMENTATION AND INCORPORATION OF THE FEMALE VOICE

WITHIN THE DOMINANTLY MALE VOICE CORPUS

OF MEDIEVAL ROMANCE COURTLY LYRIC

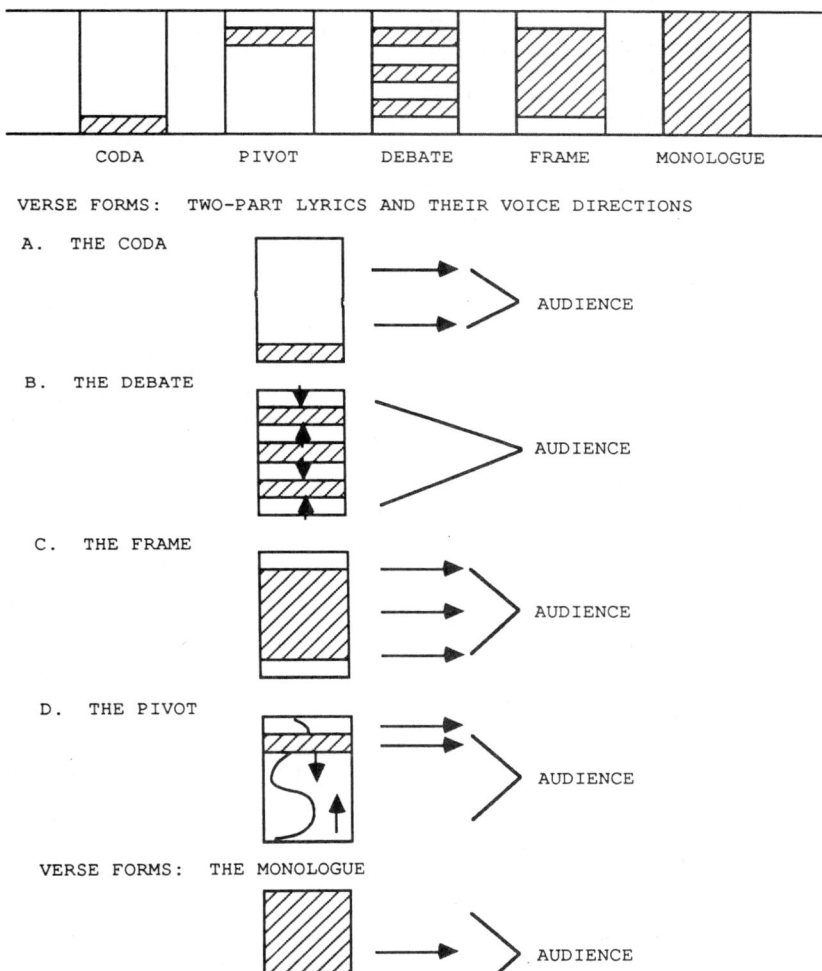

poet from the juxtaposition of the two voices, since the two speakers do not interact directly with each other in the lyric.

A different rhetorical effect is obtained with Form 2, the DEBATE. Here the female speaker appears two, three, four or more times depending on the number of strophes in the lyric. She shares half the poem, either the second half of each strophe, or alternate strophes, or, rarely, whole poems. She appears also in the tornada or tornadas. Her words are essential to the narrative line, to the dramatic resolution, and to the verbal texture throughout the lyric. Her voice, however, is in a sub-dominant position in that the male voice opens the poem and is the verbal aggressor to whom she responds. The voices are directed toward each other in the lyric and the audience in performance looks in on the dramatic encounter.

Form 3, the FRAME, is a two-part lyric in which a male voice, marked by objectivity and impersonality, introduces a female speaker. The male voice may also close the lyric, although the female voice, usually passionate in tone, may continue to the end. The effect established by this form, and it is a crucial one, is that the male speaker sets the stage and is the actual speaker throughout the lyric, although the power of mimesis lends imaginary existence to the female character.

In Form 4, the PIVOT, a male voice also introduces the female speaker, often as an "overheard" snatch of song sung by a woman who is unaware of the narrator's presence. The lyric from then on often consists of the unfolding of the theme contained in the overheard song of lyric within a lyric. The dramatic and narrative elements of the larger whole spin out of the embedded capsule or nugget which is the "pivot" on which the lyric turns.

The female voice MONOLOGUE, Form 5, must also be seen as reported or borrowed speech within courtly lyric, since the vast majority, indeed. some 90% of extant lyrics are in the male voice. Here the repertoire of the poet is the reporting voice and the female voice is a fragment or strain within the entire corpus of Romance lyric. Female speech in monologues is marked by nature symbolism, exclamatory tone, and a binary (A-B) rhyme pattern, among other markers.

The female voice used as CODA can be studied in the medieval Arabic strophic poem. the muwashsha, or "colored belt" from its alternating patterns. Linguistically, the muwashsha reflects the confluence of three cultures--Arabic, Hebrew, and Christian--that co-existed at the time of the flowering of the poem type in the eleventh and twelfth centuries, 1050-1150. Classical Arabic or Hebrew is used for the main body of the poem, but the closing lines are frequently in colloquial speech; vulgar Arabic or the Mozarabic dialect of Spanish, that is to say the Romance vernacular spoken by descendants of Christians living under Islamic rule from the eighth century. When the closing lines are in Mozarabic Spanish, they are almost exclusively in the direct speech of a young woman, who passionately proclaims her love for an Arabic master (her "habib") or her distress from love. These small "lyrics within a lyric" are of great interest to Romanists, both because they are the earliest examples of lyric poetry in Romance languages, and because they have striking formal and thematic similarities with other female speech songs in earlier poetry (Greek, notably) and with refrains and women's songs in other medieval Romance languages.[4]

Let us look at a bilingual muwashsha written c. 1065 by the Hispano-Arabic poet Abū 'Isà ibn Labbūn, of Murviedro and Toledo. The opening lines and five stanzas are typical of the amatory themes of the muwashsha, and are given in the Spanish translation, or literal version, of Garcia Gomez following the single manuscript:

> Dime: ¡Cómo se encuentran los corazones que, como sabes, fueron moldeados por los deseos y que no pueden apartarse de una flecha que viene de los ojos lánguidos?
>
> ¡Dónde está la paciencia, dónde? Y, ¡cómo podré perseverar? Amo a una gacela de dulce brama, que desacredita al sol del día. Por ella mi razón ha enloquecido e incluso he perdido mi vergüenza. No hay remedio para mí, más que en la excelencia del contento mutuo, con quien me ha castigado con la enfermedad del amor, ahora y antes.
>
> Es una gacela joven y seductora en cuyo rostro hay un jardín. Su talle, con abundante cabellera, está adornado con granados. Sus mejillas presentan jazmines que unos pendientes oscuros protejen. ¡A cuántos leones feroces, que habían sido leones de los cañaverales, el amor ha hecho probar la enfermedad que les ha conducido al borde de la muerte!
>
> ¡Oh mi censor! ¡Deja de criticarme, pues yo no soy en el amor olvidadizo! Ha cambiado con el amor mi modo de ser una gacela de dulce belleza, en cuyos labios rojos hay para mí el agua dulce y límpida, y por cuyo encanto se dirigen mis pasos. ¡Qué generosa es una mejilla estupenda de color rojo entremezclado de blanco! Si se la mira, sangra por la imaginación, ya que no porque se le muerda.

> Me gusta amarla por su fiereza y ella adora separarse de mí para mi humillación. ¡Cómo quisiera que no me recompensara por haber vendido mi religión a bajo precio, a causa de la que muestra unos andares como una rama que se dobla por su blandura, y que tiene una mirada mágica que siembra la duda, protegida por una víbora que mata! Es como una estrella que amase a otra estrella, a causa de unas perlas que brillan.
>
> Cómo simpatizo yo con aquella que fue tratada mal por su amado, cuando se separaron: él le quitó a causa de su amor el sueño, en injusticia hacia ella y hostilidad. Y ella no cesa en sus canciones de recitarle a la madre, diciendo . . .. ¡ <u>Oh, madre, mi amigo se va y no vuelve! Dime qué haré, madre, si mi pena no afloja.</u> 5

The poem is a love song. The poet announces his theme by inquiring of hearts molded by love's desires, which cannot remove the arrow flung by languid eyes. In the first stanza he declares his love for a very young girl whose brightness puts the sun to shame. His only hope is in mutual happiness. Stanza two contains a description of the beloved's physical beauty "her face is a garden" and a reference to lions in sugar cane fields which are brought to the edge of death by lovesickness. The poet defends himself against the censure of critics, and continues to sing the praises of his love's beauty, and of its effect in his imagination. (Stanza 3) The poet loves her for her wildness and cruelty; she loves to humiliate him; he has even abandoned his religion for her magical "gaze that sows doubt." She is protected by a deadly viper, and is a star among stars. (Stanza 4) The dramatic situation of the poet longing for his beloved is encapsulated in the words of the young woman introduced in the first part of Stanza 5, "How I sympathize with the one who was mistreated by her lover . . . and she did not end her songs to her mother, saying . . .." At that point, the voice shifts to the young woman introduced by the poet, and we hear her inserted song of love longing addressed to her mother/confidante whom she asks to help her with her pain.

A short consideration of the rhyme pattern and metrical composition of the <u>muwashsha</u> will help to clarify the significance of the closing lines of the poem. In its typical form, the <u>muwashsha</u> has five stanzas, each divided into two parts; the first with rhymes particular to that strophe, (the <u>ghusn</u>), and a second part (the <u>simt</u> or <u>qufl)</u>, whose rhymes are repeated in each strophe. Thus, like the Romance <u>villancico</u> or <u>rondeau</u>, the bilingual Arabic and Mozarabic Spanish poem has repeated elements throughout the lyric. If a poem begins with a preliminary simt (the repeated element) that group of lines is called a matla'; otherwise, i.e., without the preliminary repeated element, the poem is called aqra ("bald") or acephalous. Thus, the complete form of this muwashsha's rhymes is

MN/ ababab mn/ ededed mn/ efefef mn/ ghghgh mn/ ijijij mn
        1   2   3   4   5

In the fifth strophe, the first part (the ghusn, ijijij) introduces (in classical Arabic) the young woman who expresses herself in colloquial language (vulgar Arabic or Mozarabic) in the final simt (mn). This small but rhetorically very important coda is known technically as a markaz or harga, meaning "exit" or "sally." Its regular stressed syllabic beats and alternating rhymes of the A-B type dominate the rest of the poem.

    Indeed, although the themes of the muwashsha derive from Arabic poetic tradition, the elements of rhythm and rhyme seem to represent a penetration of Romance features through the influence of the poem's small Romance segment. The classical Arabic poem, the qasida, is a long poem of single lines, scanned quantitatively in any one of sixteen standard meters, but always in one rhyme throughout. It combines a love segment, the nasib, in a longer panegyric, the madih. which constitute the principal themes of the muwashsha. The supposition that the incorporated element, the Romance woman's song fragment, dominates the poem's composition is corroborated in the descriptions of contemporary critics.

    Some time before 1211, an Egyptian critic Ibn Sanā' al-Mulk described the form of the muwashsha in a treatise, Dār al-Tirāz (The House of Embroidery.)[6] We learn from Ibn Sanā' and from two other critics who left less comprehensive discussions, Ibn Bassām al-Shantarīnī and Ibn Khaldūn, that the closing lines or ḫarǧa was thought to be the alpha as well as the omega of the poem. The poet began his composition with the final lines in mind, and constructed the poem as a rebuttal to them, or a gloss, using stanzaic form and the meter of the original fragment. Improvisation on and amplification of a small text is, of course, a familiar mode of composition in homiletics and music, especially familiar to any medieval poet. Among modern critics, Julian Ribera as early as 1928 saw a Romance influence in the change from the Arabic single rhyme poem, "the string of pearls" in which each separate line claims individual attention, to the strophic poem whose ideas are given a polyrhythmic and polyrhyming organization in groups of lines.[7]

    We can now see the dialectical relationship of a discrete fragment of female voice speech to a larger male voice in the main body of the poem; a dialectic that penetrates to the very core of the composition. The polyphonic structure is a matrix out of which the poet can create many dramatic possibilities. The poet can build a poem that elaborates the message of the inserted Romance section of which the whole song will be an intensified restatement, as in our example. Or, frequently, the poet may build a poem toward which he takes an ironic and deprecating view in the closing statement. The exaggerations and conventions of courtly king-worship can be mocked or set in relief by the vulgar speech of a young woman who pays no heed to the attention-seeking metaphorical flowers of the male voice.[8] The introduction to the female speaker provides clues to the audience about the tenor of the approaching closure, and a separate study of these statements would be a valuable contribution. The poet may be in harmony with the female speaker, as in the following introduction:

> How many young women, sick with love, without
> knowing . . .
> would sing sadly, if they were in my position.
> (Sola Solé VI)

or he might present her objectively:

> A young woman did not cease complaining of the one who
> was unjust toward her . . . when the young woman saw
> him presumptuous and she was full of passion, she
> sang, for she had no hope other than to go to him.
> (Sola Solé XI)

A grossly erotic and vulgar tone in the female voice could contrast with and ironize a male voice of exquisite romantic imagery:

> You will not see me except on condition that
> you join
> my ankle bracelets to my earrings.
> (Sola Solé XLVIII)

or, to contrast with a male voice of elaborate embroidery (a refined male voice style Monroe calls "pointilliste"), she could speak with disarming simplicity and frankness:

> Come to my side, lover! If you go, the sorcerer will
> bring bad luck. Come to make love!
> (Sola Solé XVI)

The sudden and abrupt turn from refined speech in the male voice to the passionate and earthy suggestions in the female voice gives the poem a spicy, piquant flavor at the important moment of closure. The rhetorical effect of the poem is obtained by the contrast of voices. Both voices address the audience, not each other. It is in the ear of the listener that the jarring texture is assimilated into a whole meaning. Two streams of verbal performance present in the culture are brought to the consciousness of the listener in the poetic artifact. The sequential movement of a male and then a female voice becomes a single design expressive of the larger patterns of social and cultural existence. The implications of the design for our understanding of the poem in its culture will be the topic of a later chapter; it suffices here to observe the powerful, asymmetric balance of Romance and Arabic elements.

The female voice used as a responding partner in a debate or <u>tenso</u> is illustrated in Raimbaut de Vaqueiras's bilingual poem "Domna, tant vos a pregada." Written c. 1190 at the Italian court of Marquis Obizzo II Malaspina, according to its editor Joseph Linskill, it is a poem of six <u>coblas</u> <u>singulars</u> of fourteen lines each, all with seven syllables except the last of each stanza, which has four: abb abb cb cb bbbd with two <u>tornadas</u> of six lines, abbbbc. The female voice occupies stanzas two, four, six, and the second <u>tornada</u>.

    Domna, tant vos ai pregada,
    si·us platz, qu'amar me voillatz,
    qu'eu sui vostr'endomeniatz;
    quar es pros et enseingnada
    e totz bos pretz autreiatz;
    per que'm plai vostr'amistatz.
    quar es en totz faitz corteza,
    s'es mos cors en vos fermatz
    plus qu'en nuilla Genoesa,
    per qu'er merces si m'amatz;
    e pois serai meills pagatz
    que s'era mia·l ciutatz
    ab l'aver qu'es aiostatz
        dels Genoes.

    Iuiar, voi no se' corteso
    qi me chaide·ai de zò,
    que negota no·n farò;
    ance fossi voi apesso,
    vostr'amia non serò;
    certo, ia ve scanerò,
    Proenzal mal aurao;
    tal enoio ve dirò;
    sozo, mozo, escalvao!
    ni ia voi non amerò,
    qu'eu chù bello mari ò
    que voi no se', ben lo sò.
    andai via, frare, . . .
    . . . .

Domna genta et essernida,
gaia e pros e conoissens,
vailla m vostr'enseingnamenz,
quar iois e iovens vos guida,
cortesia e pretz e sens
e totz bos captenemenz;
per que·us sui fidels amaire
senes totz retenemenz,
franc, humils e merceiaire;
tant fort me destreing e·m venz
vostr'amors, que m'es plazens;
per que sera chauzimenz,
s'ieu sui vostre benvolenz
　　　e vostr'amics.

Iuiar, voi semellai mato,
qi cotal rason tegnei;
mal vignai e mal andei!
non avei sen per un gato.
per que trop me deschasei?
que mala cosa parei;
ni no volio questa cosa
si fossi fillol de rei.
credi voi que sia mosa?
mia fè, no m'averei!
si per m'amor ve chevei,
oguano morrei de frei.
tropo son de mala lei
　　　li Proensal.

Domna, no·m siatz tant fera,
que no·s cove ni s'eschai;
anz taing ben, si a vos plai,
que de mo sen vos enquera
e que·us am ab cor verai,
e vos que·m gitetz d'esmai,
qu'eu vos sui hom e servire.
quar vei e conosc e sai
quant vostra beutat remire
fresca cum rosa en mai,
qu'el mont plus bella no n sai,
per qu'ie·us am e·us amarai;
e si bona fes mi trai,
　　　sera peccatz.

Iuiar, to proensalesco,
s'eu aia gauzo de mi,
non preso un genoì,
no t'entend plui d'un Toesco
o Sardo o Barbari;
ni non ò cura de ti.
voi t'acavillar comego?
si·l saverà mi mari,

```
mal plait averai consego.
bel messer, ver e've di;
no volo questo latì,
fraello, zo ve afì
Proenzal, va, mal vestì,
    largai me star!

Domna, en estraing cossire
m'avetz mes et en esmai;
mas enquera·us preiarai
que voillatz qu'eu vos essai,
si com Provenzals o fai,
    quant es poiatz.

Iuiar, no serò contego;
possa sì te cal de mi,
meill varà, per Sant Martì,
s'andai a ser Opetì,
que dar·v à fors' un ronci,
    car sei iuiar.
```

An English version of the female speaker's Genoese dialect follows:

    2. "Juggler, you are not polite, annoying me like this. I'll certainly do nothing of the sort. I'll not be your girlfriend, I'd rather see you hanged. In truth I'll cut your throat for you, you damned Provençal. I'll tell you this much, you silly, crop-haired lout: I'll never love you. I've got a husband handsomer than you, as I well know. Off with you, brother . . . "

    4. "Juggler, talking like that you seem crazy. Bad luck to you, coming and going. You haven't the sense of a cat; why do you keep pestering me? You have a nasty look--and I don't want this thing you offer--wouldn't even if you were a king's son. You think I'm a silly girl? By my faith you'll not have me; if you've set your heart on my love you'll die of cold this year. The Provençals are a bad lot."

    6. "Juggler, as I hope to live a happy life I count on your Provençal talk less than a Genoese penny. I don't understand you any better than I would a German or a Sard or a Moor. And I don't care about you. You want to pick a fight with me? If my husband hears of it you'll have a bad time with him. I'll

tell you straight, fine sir, I want no more of this
talk; that I swear to you, brother. Go away, shabby,
Provençal; leave me be."

"Juggler, I shan't join you. If you care so much
about me you'd do better, by St. Martin, to go off to
my Lord Obizzo; perhaps he'll give you a nag since
you're a juggler."

The song is a comic "requète d'amour" of the type "praise of the unpraiseworthy." The male voice speaks in Provençal, the respected literary language of secular lyric, while the woman uses a "rather crude form of Genoese dialect."[9] One of the earliest vernacular Italian texts, the stanzas in Genoese form an important linguistic document. Although the poem resembles Marcabru's male/female tenso, "L'autrier jost' una sebissa," written fifty years before, the argument does not shift ground with the agility of the earlier lyric.[10] In that poem the knight is repulsed after a parade of reasons and offers of presents and cash. In Raimbaut's poem the knight constantly praises the lady through three long stanzas, for which he receives a constant refusal with abuse of his speech, his appearance, and his manners. But since the woman speaks in the language of an outsider's dialect, she is doubly ludicrous. The movement in Raimbaut's poem is to intensify the pleading from stanza to stanza until the knight reverses his style in the tornada, where he makes a bluntly nationalistic appeal which implies that "the Provençals do it better," (poiatz-mounted) to which she replies, along with the customary mention of his patron, a suggestion "perhaps he'll give you a nag."

As well as sexual tension, we find economic and national tensions in the poem. Instead of personal names, the two partners are identified by their place, Provence and Genoa, neighboring and rival areas rich from crusade business in Mediterranean shipping and commerce. A slur on the richness of Genoa is implied in the first stanza as the Provençal aggressor says he would be paid better with the Genoese lady than with the castle and wealth of Genoa. In the woman's second reply, she brands him as one of his nation who shares in the bad reputation so that she would be frightened to be with him "oguano morrei de frei. [tropo son de mala lei] li Proensal." His language is not as good as her money (lines 71-3) "Iuiar, to proensalesco, s'eu aia gauzo de mi, / non preso un genoi." She classes him with other despised non-Genoese; she does not understand him, "no t'entend plui d'un Toesco / o Sardo o Barbari;" Her final lines make a joke of his patron, the Marquis Obizzo II Malaspina, who was a patron of Provençal poets ("Ser Opeti" of line 94). The harsh rhymes of the first two stanzas (atz, eso/zo) and the close friction of the two-part rhyme pattern throughout the poem build a sense of localized infighting.

Indeed, the medieval debate, one of the most popular lyric forms, employs conflict as a structural and thematic principle. In many types of debate lyric (joc partit, tenso, pastorela, and the Italian contrasto) the two contending parties might carry on their alternating discourse within a single lyric, each taking one stanza or one half of a stanza, or each speaker might occupy a whole poem, in which case the debate would consist of a set of poems. The "requête d'amour" is the most frequent topic in male/female debates, although a point of courtly love theory or simply hard-hitting or lighter personal invective and competitive boasting are staples of male/male and male/female discourse. The troubadour might carry on a debate with a real woman, as happens in Provençal lyric, or create an adversary persona to match his male persona. Provençal women poets also wrote debates with male/female partners, and with all female participants. In the male/female debate poems the issue is the struggle of desire; its repression by self-restraint and its verbal sublimation.

The view that courtly lyric mediates through verbal means conflicts formerly expressed in physical combat has been put forth recently by Howard Bloch.[11] He sees the dynamics of the "poem as trial" equally in the canso and the tenso and pastorela debate forms, because in both styles the poet is "still trapped in a zealous, if sometimes farcical struggle." As the epic came more and more to picture a world weary of physical combat as a way to settle disputes, the truth that the price of violence might exceed the rewards fostered styles of literature (lyric and romance) where verbal combat in dialectical forms of poetry replaced (poetic justice?) pictures of physical violence. Debate permitted legal structures as well. Bloch writes:

> The contemporaneous and parallel development of literary and legal institutions signals the emergence of a polyvalent mental structure whose transformational effect was felt in seemingly divergent areas of cultural and social life. [12]

The strong defense of the second voice in the tenso is actually a valued offensive weapon. In military strategy until the adoption of gunpowder in the West, techniques for repelling siege or attack were constantly in demand. The transfer of this mentality to the debate style in lyric should not surprise us. In Chapter Four, the reader will find a consideration of the importance of song style to cultural change.

The female speaker in medieval debate lyric takes two divergent attitudes toward violence, and the partition of these attitudes is marked in different languages. In some areas (Provençal, Castilian, and sometimes Italian) she may be strong, vulgar, and aggressive in her own self-defense. In Old French and Galician-Portuguese, her voice is more often submissive, with laments and dolorous cries instead of vigorous self-assertion. Except in the lyrics of the women poets, the Provençal <u>trobairitz</u> (the subject of Chapter Five), the female speaker is always a <u>respondant</u> in the discourse as in the action of the narrative. The male initiates speech to which she must reply, frequently (when she is submissive) undecided between her own desire for pleasure and fear of loss. The male doctrine of legitimized aggression against women is present in many lyrics, as in Raimbaut d'Aurenga's "Assatz sai d'amor ben parlar" in the lines:

> Si voletz dompnas guazanhar
> Quan querretz que·us fassam honors
> Si·us fan avol respos avar
> Vos las prenetz a menassar;
> Et si vos fan respos peiors
> Datz lor del ponh per mieg sas nars;
> E si son bravas siatz braus!
> Ab gran mal n'auretz gran repaus[13]

The poet adds a comic deflation to his argument, however, by his confession that he does not "da lor del ponh per mieg sas nars" because he takes no part in love; he is as confused about it as anyone, so he prefers to give advice. The Genoese woman of our example lyric threatens violence twice, in her first and last stanzas. First, she will administer it, "ance fossi voi apesso . . . / certo, ia ve scanerò" and then she calls on the figure of her husband, "si·l savera me marì / mal plait averai consego." In his study of medieval thematics, <u>Personae</u> <u>and</u> <u>Poiesis</u>, Próspero Saíz reports on the arithmetics of the female responses at the close of the plot line of the Old French <u>pastourelle</u>:

> Karl Bartsch's representative collection of eighty-eight Old French <u>pastourelles</u> shows the gallant's success in forty-six and his failures in forty-two. In twenty-eight examples where he ultimately wins, the woman still makes some attempt to resist. Thus, only eighteen relate complete success with the shepherdess' consent.[14]

If the Provençal woman is vulgar and self-defensive, and the French woman relatively more submissive, the Castilian portrait of the "mountain-woman" becomes grotesque. The "vaquerisa traviesa" of the Archipreste de Hita's <u>Libro de Buen Amor</u> shows a shepherdess transformed into a cow or goatherd accosting a lost male figure crossing a mountain pass. She blocks the way, makes demands, and wants to "luchar." Frightened by her dark and imposing presence, he agrees to give gifts and to wrestle, but only after they have eaten a hearty country meal "De buen vino un quartero / Manteca de vacas mucha / Mucha queso asadero / Leche, natas, una trucha." He is completely overcome as she grabs him, "Por la moneca me prise, / Ov' a fasar lo que quiso."[15]

The framed poem is a two-part lyric in which a narrator introduces a female speaker in the first stanza; he may or may not conclude the lyric. The narrator's proximity to the female speaker permits strong contrasting tones to be heard by the audience. The male voice is cooly observant and reportorial, while the female voice is exclamatory, passionate, even obsessed. The rhetorical effect of the frame style is to emphasize the control of the female voice by the narrator; a distance is created between the audience and the female speaker so that the audience must hear her words through the observing lens of the male's eye. In fact, it is the male who is speaking, reporting female speech, and the frame weakens the illusion of female speech autonomy. The frame voice is emotionally uninvolved, or patronizingly sympathetic, whereas the female voice is exciting and warm.

All the Old French chansons de toile, the twenty-one or twenty-two (depending on the critic) narrative songs with the flavor of archaic speech and a feudal love ethic, are within the "frame song" category.[16] Of this group of lyrics, some are found in French romances, some are attributed to the poet Audefroi le Bâtard, and nine, all from the Chansonnier de Saint Germain-des-Prés, are anonymous. One of the latter group is "Oriolanz en haut solier," a poem of nine stanzas in the octosyllabic line. Each stanza has a two-line refrain:

    Oriolanz en haut solier
    sospirant prist a lermoier
    et regrate son dru Helier:
    --Amis, trop vos font esloignier
    de moi felon et losengier.
    Deus, tant par vient sa joie lente
    a celui cui ele atalente!

    Amis, bels douz amis Helier,
    qant me membre de l'embracier,
    de l'acoler et dou baisier,
    dou dolz parlemant senz noisier,
    coment me puis vivre lassier!

    Amis je vos fis esloignier
    de moi plus que li losengier.
    kant je onques vos fis dangier,
    de m'amor vos fis estrangier.
    or en recoi si dur loiier.

> Amis, la nuit en mon couchier,
> en dormant vos cuit embracier.
> Et qant g'i fail au resveillier,
> nule riens ne m'i puet aidier.
> Lors me reprent au sohaidier.
>
> Amis, or voil a Deu proier,
> s'il me doit jamais conseillier,
> que je vos voie senz targier;
> mais a ceu vient plus d'encombrier
> dont on a plus grant desirrier."
>
> Que ke la bele fait ses criz,
> Heliers est de cort departiz.
> Vient chevalchant par un lairiz,
> si a les douz plainz entroiz:
> durement s'en est resjoiz.
>
> La bele sosleva son vis:
> voit / ke c'est Heliers ses amis.
> Baisier et acoler l'a pris,
> si l'a entre ses beax braz mis:
> assez i ot jué et ris.
>
> Oriolanz li dist: —Amis,
> malgré losengeors chaitis
> estes vos or de moi saisiz.
> Or parleront a lor devis
> et nos ferons toz noz plaisirs."
>
> Ne sai que plus vos en devis:
> ensi avengne a toz amis!
> et je, qui ceste chancon fis
> sor la rive de mer pansis,
> comanz a deu bele Aelis.   (R1312; 1275)[17]

The narrator sets the stage; the young Oriolanz is in an upstairs room sighing and crying because she misses her lover Helier. Without recognizing the narrator, Oriolanz begins her lament, which occupies the last two lines of stanza one and all of stanzas two, three, four and five. As a signal of female speech, each stanza begins with her address to her lover, "Amis." First she blames an outside cause ("felon et losengier") for his absence; then, after fond recollections of his embrace, she confesses guilt and unhappiness that she sent him away ("vos fis dangier"). She dreams of his love and will pray to God that she will see him soon. In stanzas six, seven, and eight the narrator reports the whereabouts of the lover and his return after he hears the lament of his beloved. Oriolanz welcomes him back in direct speech, again using the address. "Amis," in stanza eight, and the narrator closes the poem with words of his own that he does not know what else to tell about them. He recommends to God a woman "Aelis," perhaps his own lady to whom he may be sending the song as a cautionary tale.

In three lyrics from the Sicilian corpus we can see the rhetorical effect of the cool male voice introducing a warm female voice by means of the "frame." In the first (a dialogue of the lady with the God of Love) the narrator begins with a statement of fact

>L'amor fa una donna amare.
>Dice: "Lassa, com faragio?"[18]

about women and love, a tautology that has little sense, but which establishes the tone of rational statement in the male voice, serving as contrast to the female voice response "Lassa," a "primary" exclamation which transcribes feeling directly by exhalation of breath. Then her "com faragio?" signals her helplessness and sense of emotional urgency. In many forms in Romance lyric the phrase "What shall I do?" (Que ferai-je? Qué ferai yo?) is a topos of female speech and signals to the audience the convention of the lamenting, crisis-ridden female speaker.

In the second, (a mother-daughter dialogue).

>Part'io mi cavalcava
>audivi una donzella.
>forre si lamenrava
>dicea: "oi madre bella,
>lungo tempo e passato
>ch'io degio aver marito . . .[19]

the narrator/knight identifies himself as one who "went out riding" and came upon a woman lamenting loudly. She addresses her mother (no explanation is given for the presence of mother and daughter within earshot of a passing horseman) with a "primary" exclamation "oi," and the lament that she should have been married long ago, probably indicating to the audience that she is pregnant.

In the third lyric, the male narrator takes the persona of the woman's lover to whom she makes a cry for help to save her from the marriage to an older man that her family is forcing her into. With the impersonality that is typical of male voice opening lines in the "frame" style, he refuses to rescue her, counseling her instead to marry the older man, but to keep him as her lover. His lines to the audience that speak of her in the third person "quella cui agio amata" and "fecemi grande lamento" establish his tone of aloof non-participation in her crisis:

> L'altr'ieri fui in parlamento
> con quella cui agio amata;
> fecemi grande lamento,
> c'a forza fui maritata;
> e dissemi: "Drudo mio,
> merzè, ti chero, or m'aiuta 20

The interrupted pattern of her speech sets an emotional tone of hesitation and breathlessness. The four fragments of her speech ("Lover--please--I beg you--help me") contrast to his one long introductory sentence that stretches out over four lines and a half in a flowing development. Thus the poet sets the criteria for male and female speech contrast, a speech difference made clear to the audience from the first stanza of the frame lyric with its juxtaposition of a cool, objective onlooker to a subjective voice of experience lived by the speaking woman.

The female speaker used as a pivot in a dramatic narrative may be seen in the Old French lyric "Quant la douce saisons fine."

> Quant la douce saisons fine,
> que li fel yvers revient,
> que flors et fuelle decline,
> que ces oiselez ne tient
> de chanter en bois n'en broil,
> en chantant, si com je soil,
> toz seus mon chemin erroie;
> si oï pres d'une voie
> chanter la bele Aielot:
> "<u>Dorenlot, j'aim bien Guiot!</u>
> <u>Toz mes cuers a lui s'ottroie</u>."
>
> Grant joie fait la meschine,
> quant de Guiot li sovient.
> Je li dis: "Amie fine,
> cil vos saut qui tot maintient!
> Vostre amor desir et voil;
> a vos servir toz m'acoil;
> se daingniez que vostre soie,
> ceyntur vos donrai de soie;
> si laissiez cel vilain sot,
> dorenlot, c'ainz ne vos sot
> bien amer ne faire joie."
>
> "Sire, or m'avez essaiee,
> mais pou i avez conquis;
> mainte autre en avez proiee,
> si ne l'avez pas apris,
> nen ici ne lo lairois.
> N'est pas li cuers si destrois,
> con il pert a la parole.

>   Tels baise feme et acole,
>   qui ne l'aime tant ne quant.
>   Dorenlot, alez avant,
>   ja ne me troverez fole!"[21]

The poem has three stanzas in the rhyme scheme a b a b c c d d e e d, with seven syllables to the line. The final two lines of the first stanza (c d) contain the emotional core of the poem, a fragment of direct female speech that acts as a pivot around which the action turns:

>   Dorenlot, j'aim bien Guiot!
>   Toz mes cuers a lui s'ottroie.

The poem is a gloss on these two lines, an "amplificatio" because nothing new is added that is not in the kernel of female speech. The message of the small part is spun out, tested, consented, debated, and ratified as a valid statement. Stanza one, a single grammatical entity, begins with a reverse nature introduction heralding loss of love. Summer is ended, flowers and leaves fall, and birds stop singing. The knight, alone on his path, hears a young woman singing of her love. She pledges her heart to be true to her Guiot. Stanza two begins with a male voice paraphrase of the pivot lines in prosaic, third person speech, "Grant joie fait la meschine, quant de Guiot li sovient." The factual restatement of the woman's personal exclamation of feeling establishes the male voice as a reporting, observing voice. He offers love and gifts, on the condition that she renounce her vow, i.e., that she leave her country bumpkin, the "vilain sot." Stanza three gives her retort in a sermonette about men who hug and kiss without loving. She has been tested before and is not to be won away from her love. Infidelity is equated with folly. We are close to a temptation scene in a buccolic setting with a rustic Adam and Eve and a snaky knight. Adam is off-stage and Eve resists the blandishments of the cool and calculating tempter. Both "Aielot" and "Guiot" are stock names found in many lyrics, the "ot" suffix being a term of endearment still in use today. The poem's dialectic sets the small fragment of direct female speech against a longer development that challenges its truth.

The tone of the woman's voice in the pivot position is one of high spirits and self-glorification. The anonymous dance songs exhibit these qualities, with adjectives such as "coindeta," "savoureuse," "jolivete" used by women speakers about themselves. Perhaps the small fragments of incorporated material, the "pivots" are refrains or parts of a much larger body of song now lost. They certainly indicate a wholesome, self-approving attitude on the part of the woman speaker. One sings:

> J'ai amoretes a mon gre
> S'en sui plus jolivete assez.[22]

Another is confident of the good benefits of her love:

> Cil doit bien grant joie avoir
> Qui j'ai m'amor donee.[23]

Another is frankly joyous in her love:

> Saderla don!
> Tant fait bon
> dormir lez le buissonet.[24]

The snatch of song inserted as a pivot provides a vivid emotional core around which a lyric can be constructed. In responding to her voice, the male speaker as narrator can set a scene, comment on her words and paraphrase them in a more sober, rational style.

A whole song could become a pivot in a courtly romance. As the courtly narrative in vernacular Romance languages began, it borrowed from lyric at both the thematic and the structural levels. Songs were commonly embedded in the early romances. In several, the song seems to have been the prior creation, because the narrative expands the details of the song with compositional techniques of amplificatio. Of the twenty-one remaining chansons de toile, seven appear in romances, their only surviving manuscript location. In a romance, the woman's song slows the action by its change of style, interrupting the forward flow of narrative or dramatic lyric. In stopping time, the woman's song induces nostalgia, providing a window on a timeless moment. It is the still center of the larger canvas of action. Since it comes after the introduction and before the main events of the literary work, it acts as a small intermission, and may be related to performance, allowing the audience a retrospective moment to adjust to the new material presented. It may be a spatial and temporal metaphor for the distance that separates the two voices, with the greater assuming superiority over the smaller voice. By permitting a small view of the female world, the poet creates reflection, a dédoublement of consciousness to insure the validity of his work.

Henri d'Andeli's Lai d'Aristote illustrates the use of a female voice as a pivot in narrative.[25] The tale is from the East: Aristotle has ordered his pupil Alexander to avoid feminine companionship and physical contact with women. To overcome the hated restriction, Alexander and his mistress plan for her to seduce Aristotle by song. After a series of male voice songs fails to move him, the mistress sings a chanson de toile. "En un vergier, lez une fontenele," and the venerable, white-haired, and foolish philosopher capitulates, agreeing to let Alexander's mistress ride

piggyback while he is on all fours in the courtyard. The
song's erotic content gave secular lyric a poor reputation
with religious authority. It is a <u>malmariée</u> story in six
stanzas, whose six lines rhyme AAAABB. In the first stanza
the setting and diction provide reminders of epic style and
theme:

> En un vergier, lez une fontenele
> dont clere est l'onde et blanche la gravele
> siet fille a roi, sa main a sa maxele
> En sospirant son doux ami rapele:
> --Ae, cuens Guis amis
> la vostre amors me tout solaz et ris!

Her husband hears her lament, and severely beats her for her
disturbance. But he is afraid of her father the king, and
realizes he has made a mistake:

> Li mals mariz en oi la deplainte
> Entre el vergier, sa corroie a desceinte
> Tant la bati a'ele en fu perse et tainte:
> entre ses piez por pou ne l'a estainte
> --Ae, cuens Guis amis
> la vostre amors me tout solaz et ris!

> Li mals mariz, qant il l'ot laidangie,
> Il s'en repent, car ot fait folie,
> car il fu ja de son pere maisnie,
> Bien seit 'ele est fille a roi, koi u'il die
> --Ae, cuens Guis amis,
> la vostre amors me tout solaz et ris!

She prays to God, who sends her lover:

> --Bels sire doux, ja m'avez vos formee;
> donez moi, sire, que ne sois obliee
> ke mes amis revengne ainz la vespree
> --Ae, cuens Guis amis,
> la vostre amors me tout solaz et ris![26]
> (R594; 109.4/265.674)

The final stanza shows the lover and young wife weeping
under a tree. This song, in the context of the story, was
considered more lascivious than the male-voice songs. It
provided the strong aphrodisiac required to move the aged
philosopher.

   There is a sense in which the female voice is a pivot
for all of courtly lyric in medieval Romance languages, an
element upon which male dominated courtly literature built
the secular love song that would become the normative voice
in lyric poetry for many centuries. Female speech provided
a style against which male speech could distinguish itself,
and then becoming conscious of itself, divorce itself and
stand alone, as Le Gentil has suggested. We have seen the

girl's song in Mozarabic Spanish to be the emotional core around which the poet wove the strands of the Arabic muwashsha. Likewise, in the other two-voice verse forms, the debate, frame, and pivot, the male poet's dominant voice marks female speech as different and sub-dominant. But how, in a monologue, when the female speaker is the single voice throughout the lyric, does the poet create gender differentiation? In the concluding part of this chapter, we will examine in detail the formal qualities of female speech such as nature imagery, tone, fragmentation by refrain types, and rhyme patterns; all means employed by the troubadour in medieval Romance lyric. By marking the female voice as a special type, the male voice reserved for itself qualities that would be identified with a dominant speech style. By literally contradicting the female speech type, the poet achieved the creation of the sounds and forms that would prevail in European culture.

When we speak of the poet "marking" female personae in dramatic lyric with special characteristics, we should be aware that the poet is not inventing differences out of his unassisted imagination. From the beginning of scientific linguistic studies in this century, gender difference in human speech has been a recognized fact. Gender is universally distinguishable in human speech.[27] In some societies, parts of the vocabulary are reserved for men, others for women; this trait can become so exaggerated in certain tribes that a quite different language is used by each sex. Also, specialists have noted that women's speech tends to preserve archaic patterns in diction and rhythm. Women often live in a restricted area, while the more mobile men may cultivate the speech of an invader, or, if they are conquerers, of an invaded people. Intonation differs by gender. Women tend to use a plaintive or begging intonation of rising inflection at the end of sentences. They also use more frequent interrogations, fewer commands. Exclamation is a trait of female speech, as well as tentativeness and hesitation. Current research in sociolinguistics, which continues the pioneer work of Jesperson, Sapir, Whorf, and Haas, provides abundant and fascinating data on the gender marking of human speech.[28] Poets, then, who are by their craft and native talents tuned to nuances of speech in their communities, employ specific verbal textures to control the dramatic effects of their female personae.

By no means all, but a significant number of female voice monologues are carriers of folkloric nature images that may be part of a common stock of Indo-European folkmotifs, diffused over much of Europe. Medieval Romance imagery that seems clearly Biblical, like the stags and mountains from the Song of Songs, is now thought by scholars to pre-date that compilation of wedding songs. The similarities of Slavonic and Romance animal and human symbology seem to point to a common source further back than the

Hebrew. Alan Deyermond, in an article of wide scope, "Pero Meogo's Stags and Fountains," delineates the folkloric identification of natural elements and human experience in examples from Galician-Portuguese and other female voice lyrics.[29] The cold fountain being stirred by the stag, the wind coming through an open door, the waves of Vigo Bay are images of sexual experience thinly veiled. The young woman often addresses the natural force with direct speech, as here, to the pines:

> --Ai, flores, ai, flores do verde pino,
> se sabedes novas do meu amigo?
> Ai, Deus, e u e?[30]

or she may call to the mountain doe, symbol of animal power:

> Ai, cervas do monte, vin-vos preguntar:
> foi-se o meu amigo e, se la tardar,
> que farei, velidas?[31]

and, in the beautiful "boat song," or <u>barcarola</u> of Martim Codax, she calls to the waves:

> Ondas do mar de Vigo,
> se vistes meu amigo!
> E ai, Deus, se verra cedo![32]

or she may talk of the wind raising her clothes as in King Dinis' lyric:

> Vai lavar camisas
> (levantou-s alva);
> o vento lhas desvia
> em o alto.[33]

Hair being washed in the cold stream is an image of the sexual encounter in the lyric of Pero Meogo:

> [Levou-s'a louçana],
> levou-s'a velida;
> vai lavar cabelos
> na fontana fria,
>   leda dos amores,
>   dos amores leda.[34]

In female voice lyrics of this type, then, it seems clear that the medieval poet continued the ancient poetic identification of sexual potency and natural elements: waves, wind, pine trees and animals. Likewise, the female speaker's response to the powerful sexual experience shows an equally characteristic linguistic expression. Speech qualities that have been described as "spontaneous," "vivid," "fresh," and "direct" are achieved by the use of such means as exclamation, direct appeal to natural forces, incantation (close repetition of small elements) and simple A-B rhymes. We have already noted the formulaic expression in female speech, "Que ferai-je?" a phrase that combines interrogation, exclamation, and brief intensity; all hallmarks of female speech. Perhaps the ḫarǧa XXXIX, "What shall I do, mother? My lover is at the door!" may be called the quintessence of female speech character in medieval Romance lyric. Its appeal is in its immediate crisis, but the sociolinguistic importance is in the use of the Arabic "habib" meaning the lover. The Mozarabic Spanish speaker is dealing with a member of a superior class, a true analogue for the culture that sees "every lover as a soldier." The female speaker of Galician-Portuguese cantigas de amigo calls out for help to God, to saints, to objects of clothing, to friends, and to the mother. In the beautiful lyric of Pero Gonçalves Porto Carreiro, "Par Deus, coitada vivo," we hear these speech elements of the female voice: direct address to inanimate objects, appeal for help from the community, formulaic exclamation of helplessness. These are the means by which the poet achieves the female voice pathos, the immediacy of tone, the "spontaneity" that has attracted generations of critics:

> Par Deus, coitada vivo:
> pois non ven meu amigo:
> pois non vem, que farei?
> meus cabelos, con sirgo
> eu non vos liarei.
>
> Pois non ven de Castela,
> non é viv', ai mesela.
> ou mi-o detem el-rei:
> mias toucas da Estela.
> eu non vos tragerei.
>
> Pero m'eu leda semelho,
> non me sei dar conselho;
> amigas, que farei?
> en vos, ai meu espelho,
> eu non me veerei.
>
> Estas dôas mui belas
> el mi-as deu, ai donzelas,
> non vo-las negarei:
> mias cintas das fivelas,
> eu non vos cingerei.[35]

In Stanza one, the speaker voices her distress; the king has taken her lover away. She uses the conventional "que farei?" and speaks to her hair some words of comfort; she will not bind them up, but will leave them loose (a symbol of mourning). In Stanza two she gives details about her lover's absence; he has gone away to Castile, and she will will not wear the special gown, the toucas. In Stanza three, after another expression of despair, she addresses her mirror. She cannot bear to see her image in it and will not look at it. In Stanza four she considers the gifts her lover has given her, but will not wear the lovely belt. The painful separation from her love, a separation motivated by concerns of male political life, is a source of many negative feelings for her. Her intimate contact, expressed by personification and direct address with the articles of her physical and emotional life (hair, clothing, mirror, and gifts), places her in the world of primitive magic where objects and feelings are unified.

The incantatory effect of female speech in lyric is best illustrated by the use of refrains, particularly in Galician-Portuguese monologues in the female voice. Indeed, the refrain has long been recognized as a notable feature of women's songs, and its absence is a distinguishing feature of the sonnet, the verse form that became the literary standard for European male voice lyric in the centuries following the period of this study. The "popular" male voice lyric never totally abandoned the refrain. Literally a re-breaking, from "refrangere," the refrain is a fragmenting device, a regular pattern of interruption in dance songs, <u>albas</u>, and other songs of a popular and traditional character. It is smaller and brighter than the stanza it follows. A staple of choral singing, it represents the community, since the group sings the refrain while the leader sings the verses. It often contains open vowels and nonsense syllables, exclamations, and formulaic phrases:

>   odeli odeli odeli o!
>   dieus! amors m'ont navrei a mort.[36]
>
>   chibera la chibele, douz amis
>   chibera la chibele, soiez jolis.[37]
>
>   j'ai ameit et amerai
>   he! dorenlot! et s'aimme aincor
>   deus! de jolif cuer mignot.[38]

Critics take the refrain to be a source of information on the possibility of a stock of now lost popular material, much of it in the female voice. The same refrain will appear in several songs, or a poet narrator will say, "I do not remember the whole song" when he represents a fragment. Margit Frenk Alatorre demonstrates similarities between Mozarabic Spanish harǧas and Old French refrains in her article "Jaryas mozarabes y estribillos françeses."[39] In both literatures, the expression of feeling is direct and vivid:

>   les mamelettes me poignent
>   Je ferai novel amors.⁴⁰
>
>   Au cuer les ai, les jolis malz:
>   comment en guariroie?⁴¹
>
>   Non dormireyo, mama,
>   a rayo de manana:
>   bon Abū-l-Qasīm,
>   la faye de matraña.⁴²

Nico Van Den Boogaard makes the suggestion, in his useful collection of Old French refrains, that the refrain is a separate poetic genre, albeit a parasite in symbiotic dependence on the poem.⁴³ The sequel to his book of refrains, an extended interpretation, is eagerly awaited.

The relationship of the refrain to the poem, however, is not uniform; indeed, it shifts and slips around in Protean fashion. Sometimes it guards its autonomy and sense of self-definition. It can act then as a distancing device. In other lyrics it is first an outgrowth of the thought of the first stanza, after which it becomes more distant in meaning, pleasant for its musical values. In many lyrics it changes in the final stanza to give the security of closure. The speaker of the refrain may not be the same as the poem's narrator. The refrain speaker may represent the community of singers, or the leading or secondary character in the dramatic story.

The display of refrain types in the Galician-Portuguese cantigas de amigo is very rich. We can appreciate the emotional tone they give to the female voice if we compare two lyrics, both attributed to King Dinis of Portugal, in the male and female voice styles. Of this poet's one hundred and thirty-three extant lyrics, seventy-three are men's love songs, fifty are women's voice songs, and ten are songs of scorn and invective (cantigas d'escarnho e mal dizer. Typical of his male voice songs is the following, a tongue-in-cheek questioning of a lady who is causing him grief:

>   Que razon cuydades vós, mha senhor,
>   dar a Deus, quand' ant'El fordes, por mi.
>   que matades, que vos non mereci
>   outro mal, se non se vos ey amor,
>   aquel mayor que vo' l'eu poss' aver,
>   ou que salva lhi cuydades fazer
>   da mha morte, poys per vós morto for?
>
>   Ca na mha morte non á [i] razon
>   bõa que ant'El possades mostrar,
>   des y non o er podedes enganar,

>   ca El sabe ben quam de coraçon
>   vos eu am' e [que] nunca vos errey
>   e por en quen tal feyto faz ben sey
>   que en deus nunca pod' achar perdon
>
>   Ca de pran Deus non vos perdoará
>   a mha morte, ca El sabe mui ben
>   ca sempre foy meu saber e meu sen
>   en vos servir; er sabe mui ben [já]
>   que nunca vos mereci por que tal
>   morte per vós ouvesse, por en mal,
>   vos será, quand' ant'El formos alá.[44]

In a manner recalling the lyric as inquest, commented by Bloch, Dinis' poet-lover takes God for the judge, himself as plaintiff and the lady as defendant. She will have to justify her treatment of him before the High Court when he dies of love. The poem's reasoning tone, syntax of subordinate clauses and textual density with new material in each line (although phrases are repeated) and chiastic rhyme scheme <u>abbacca</u> of quatrain and tercet mark it as the goal toward which the male voice lyric style is tending. This tone will flower in later centuries in the Italian, French, and English sonnet.

The woman's song in Dinis' repertoire, on the other hand, shows a different quality. Here are refrains, in 49 out of 50 lyrics, and a movement toward incantation and exclamation without reasoning or judgement. The following song is a style which appears, with one or two exceptions, only in the woman's voice:

>   Ai, flores, ai, flores do verde pîo,
>   sabedes novas do meu amigo?
>   ai, Deus, e u é?
>
>   Ai, flores, ai flores do verde ramo,
>   se sabedes novas do meu amado?
>   ai, Deus e u é?
>
>   Se sabedes novas do meu amigo,
>   aquel que mentiu do que pôs comigo?
>   ai, Deus, e u é?
>
>   Se sabedes novas do meu amado
>   aquel que mentiu do que mi á jurado?
>   ai, Deus, e u é?
>
>   --Vós me preguntades polo voss' amigo?
>   E eu ben vos digo que é sá e vivo:
>   ai, Deus, e u é?

>   Vós me preguntades polo voss' amado?
>   E eu ben vos digo que é viv' e sâo:
>   ai, Deus, e u é?
>
>   E eu ben vos digo que é sâ' e vivo
>   e seera vosc' ant' o prazo saido:
>   ai, Deus, e u é?
>
>   E eu ben vos digo que é viv' e sâo
>   e s/e/erá vosc' ant' o prazo passado:
>   ai, Deus, e u é?[45]

This song type is the most complicated and delicate of the binary lyric patterns. It is a <u>cosaute</u> (or dance song, literally "jumping together"), and it has been the subject of much analysis and interpretation.[46] Fewer in number than other female voice lyrics, these poems are more brilliant in their poetic effect. Their interlacing repetitions of whole lines, and rhymes effected with the change of a single vowel within a word are achievements of a high order. Not only have modern critics been interested in their patterns and symbolic content, but modern poets have imitated their style. Typically they have six stanzas, though often more or less, of three lines with a shorter third line in many cases. Line length may vary from eight to eleven or more syllables in patterns such as 11-11-3, 11-11-8, 8-8-8. The "leisured and hypnotic movement" of the <u>cosaute</u> is a medieval minimalist art form. In his <u>The Spanish Traditional Lyric</u>, J. G. Cummins writes of it:

> The thematic content, often no greater than that condensed in a two or three line <u>estribillo</u> elsewhere, is spun out in an alternating pattern of advance and regression, in which each stanza picks up and slightly develops ideas already expressed, so that the effect is that of a doubly woven chain . . .[47]

In the two preceeding examples, we have seen the male voice <u>mestría</u> style in the pattern <u>abbacca deedffd ghghiih,</u> and the female voice <u>cosaute</u> style in the pattern <u>aaB aaB aaB aaB aaB aaB aaB aaB</u>. These styles represent the extremes of difference between male and female song patterns in Galician-Portuguese lyric of this period. There is, however, a major song pattern that is common to both male and female voice lyrics. It has a six-line stanza of <u>abbacc</u>, and often the last two lines are a refrain in the three stanzas of the lyric. This, along with the <u>mestría</u> style above, is the standard form for male voice songs. With almost no exceptions, the male voice song has no more than the two-line refrain repetition. The two following examples show this common form, first in the male voice and then in the female voice. The first is a <u>cantiga de amor</u> of Joan

Garcia de Guilhade in which the poet uses his favored images of eyes, sight, and love:

> Vi oj' eu donas muy ben parecer
> e de muy bon prez e de muy bon sen,
> e muyt' amigas son de todo ben:
> mays d' ûa moça vos quero dizer:
> de parecer venceu quantas achou
> i a moça que x' agora chegou.
>
> Cuydava-m' eu que non avian par
> de parecer as donas que eu vi,
> atan ben me parecian alí;
> mays, po[y]-la moça filhou seu logar,
> De parecer venceu quantas achou
> i a moça que x' agora chegou.
>
> Que feramente as todas venceu
> a mocelia en pouca sazon!
> De parecer todas vençudas (?) son;
> mays, poy-la moça alí pareceu,
> de parecer venceu quanta[s] achou
> i a moça que x' agora chegou.

A song in the same pattern in the female voice is "Ora veerie, amiga, que fará," of Joan Baveca, in which the young woman tells that her lover lost her because he did not know how to keep the "guardians" in ignorance:

> Ora veerei, amiga, que fará
> o meu amigo, que non quis creer
> o que lh'eu dix'e soube-me perder,
> ca de tal guisa me guardam d'el ja
>   que non ei eu poder de fazer ren
>   por el, mais esto buscou el mui ben.
>
> El quis comprir sempre seu coraçon
> e soub'assi sa fazenda trager
> que tod'ome nos podia'ntender,
> e pois aquestas guardas tantas son
>   que non ei /eu/ poder de fazer ren
>   por el, mais esto buscou el mui ben.
>
> E, pero lh'eu já queira des aqui
> o maior ben que lhi possa querer.
> por non poder. non lhi farei prazer,
> e digo-vos que me guardan assi
>   que non ei eu poder de fazer ren
>   Por el, mais esto buscou el mui bem.
>
> E. vedes vós, assi conteç'a quen
> non sab'andar en tal preito con sen.[49]

The range of similarities and differences in male and female voice rhyme patterns may be visualized in the following chart:

Figure 2

CANTIGAS DE AMIGO (Female Voice Forms)								CANTIGAS DE AMOR (Male Voice Forms)		
a	a	a	a	a	a	a		a	a	a
a	a	a	a	b	a	a		b	b	b
b	a	b	b	a	b	a		b	b	b
	b	b	b	b	b	b		a	a	a
		b	b	a		b		c	c	c
			b	a		b		c	c	c
				a						a

BINARY RHYMES	AREA OF OVERLAP	CHIASTIC RHYMES

When we examine refrains in female voice songs more closely, we find a range of uses and poetic effects. A refrain may consist of one word only, a device (anaphora) familiar to writers of prose as well as poetry. In the following lyric of Lourenço jograr, the single word has semantic importance:

> Amiga, des que meu amigo vi,
> el por mi morr'e eu ando des i
> namorada.
>
> Des que o vi, primeiro lhi falei,
> el por mi morr'e eu ando por en
> namorada.[50]

The adjective namorada ("in love") has a setting appropriate to its key meaning in the lyric. Other single word refrain lines illustrate the tendency to fragment and imbed the female voice, in this case within the poem itself in a lyric of Fernan Rodriguez de Calheiros:

> Que farei agor', amigo?
> pois que non queredes migo
> viver,
> ça non poss'eu al ben querer.[51]

The four stanzas of this lyric are a meditation on the theme of life and death. The word "viver" is made to stand alone, but with an altered semantic relationship to the preceding

line in each stanza. The same poet uses the pattern again
with a similar rhetorical effect:

> Agora vẽo [o] meu amigo
> a quer-se loqu'ir e non quer migo
> 　　　estar;
> ave-l'ei j'á sempr'a desejar.[52]

One line refrains emphasize the close play of repetitions as
in the lyric of six stanzas of AAB rhyme by Fernand' Esquio:

> Vaiamos, irmãa, vaiamos dormir
> [en] nas ribas do lago, u eu andar vi
> 　　　a las aves meu amigo.
>
> Vaiamos, irmãa, vaiamos folgar
> [en] nas ribas do lago, u eu vi andar
> 　　　a las aves meu amigo.[53]

Or, a one-line refrain may be imbedded in the stanza in a
sort of rondo form ababa, as in the following lyric of Don
Afonso Sanches:

> Dizia la fremosinha:
> 　　ai, Deus, val!
> Com'estou d'amor ferida!
> 　　ai, Deus, val!
> Com'estou d'amor ferida![54]

In this four stanza lyric, the first two stanzas are in a
male voice, making the lyric a "frame" song. The rhyme
pattern of only two elements in a relation of opposition,
not crossing, so typical of the female voice, may be seen in
this last example of one-line refrains, a three stanza lyric
of AAAB rhyme:

> Foi-s'o meu amigo d'aqui noutro dia
> coitad'e sanhud'e non soub'eu ça s'ia,
> mais, já que o sei, e por santa Maria
> 　　e que farei eu, louçaa?[55]

Here we find the topos "que ferei eu?" and the word of
self-praise "louçaa" both typical marks of the female voice
in traditional lyric style.

　　Two-line refrains in the female voice are similar to the
example given above for the male voice lyric; variation,
however, is so frequent that it becomes a principle. The
tendency is to dramatize the two-line refrain, as we can see
in the three following examples. First, a daughter speaks
to her mother; she fears she has lost her lover through her
pride and disobedience. The daughter speaks through the
four stanzas of four lines, in the aabb rhyme pattern:

> Perdud'ei, madre, cuid'eu, meu amigo;
> macar m'el viu, sol non quis falar migo,
> e mia sobervia mi'o tolheu,
> que fiz o que m'el defendeu.[56]

Her confession in the refrain fits each stanza of the six in a slightly different semantic relationship. Second, the refrain may be an interrogation arising from the meaning of the stanza, as spoken by the young woman:

> Ir-vos queredes, amigo, d'aquem
> e dizedes-mi vos que vos quis'eu
> que faledes ante comigu'e, meu
> amigo, dizede ora ua ren:
>   como farei eu fan gran(de) prazer
>   a quen mi tan gran pesar quer fazer?[57]

In each stanza, the refrain continues the thought of the dilemma she is expressing. The following lyric, well-known for both its folkloric content and its *leixa-pren* (drop and pick up) technique, has a two-line refrain with an interior chiastic structure of its own:

> [Levou-s'a louçana],
> levou-s'a velida;
> vai lavar cabelos
> na fontana fria
>   leda dos amores,
>   dos amores leda.[58]

Refrains with three lines continue the dramatizing nature of the two-line variations, with frequent use of interrogative. The refrain may be equal to the stanza in semantic weight and contain its own pattern of repetitions as we see in the following lyric in the rhyme scheme AABBB:

> Amigo, se ben ajades,
> rogo-vos que mi digades:
>   por que non vivedes migo,
>   meu conselhle meu amigo;
>   por que non vivedes migo?[59]

A three-line refrain, again with its own interior repetition, fits the line that introduces it in a new way with each repetition in a lyric by Pero d'Ardia. The introductory line contains the narrative kernel of the lyric and has its own progression:

> 1.   "e por en, se quiser, ande"
> 2.   "se quiser, e, se non, ande"
> 3.   "e comigu'e ala x'ande"
> 4.   "mais non quer'eu, e el ande"[60]

to which the refrain replies:

>   sanhud'e non mi-o demande;
>   quant'el quiser atant'ande
>   sanhud'e non mi-o demande. 61

The close linking of introductory line and refrain is marked by identical rhyme, "ande," making a four-line sequence.

Four-line refrains are marked by monorhyme, which is, as we saw in the section on the *coda*, a characteristic of Arabic poetry. It often indicates a dance rhythm when used in short lines in Romance lyric, and is characteristic of the *estampida* of which Raimbaut de Vaqeiras' "Kalenda maya" is a famous example. The following example is a stanza from a "romaría" or pilgrimage song by Golpardo, in which a young woman protests that her mother watches her too closely at a religious festival:

>   Mal fac'eu, velida, que ora non vou
>   ver meu amigo, pois que me mandou
>   que foss'(oj')eu con el ena sagraçon
>   fazer oraçon
>   a San Treeçon
>   d'ir ei coraçon
>   a San Treeçon. 62

A lyric of Gonçalo Eanes do Vinhal uses word repetition to blend the rhyme pattern AAAA and ABAB in the four-line refrain:

>   Que leda que oj'eu sejo
>   por que mi enviou dizer
>   ça non ven con gran desejo
>   coitado d'u foi viver
>   ai, dona', lo meu amigo
>   se non por falar conmigo;
>   nen ven por al meu amigo
>   se non por falar conmigo. 63

A woman's complaint by Joao Servando shows the same pattern in the refrain:

>   ça non ei, sen vos, a veer
>   amigo, ond'eu aja prazer;
>   e com'ei, sen vos, a veer
>   ond'eu aja nen ũa prazer? 64

A variation of the principle of monorhyme in long refrains is the lyric "Mal me tragedes, ai filha," in which a mother addresses her daughter:

> Mal me tragedes, ai filha,
> porque quer'aver amigo
> e pois eu con vosso medo
> non o ei, nen e comigo,
> > non ajade-la mia graça
> > e de-vos Deus, ai mia filha,
> > filha que vos assi faça
> > filha que vos assi faça.⁶⁵

The word "filha" (the <u>a</u> rhyme word) is picked up in the refrain from the first line of the first stanza; subsequent stanzas have the word "amigo" (rhyme word <u>b</u>) so that the pattern of rhymes:

    1) abcb dadd
    2) befe dadd
    3) bghg dadd
    4) biji dadd

balances the words "amigo" and "filha" through the lyric. We should also note that the line "filha que vos assi faça" addressed to "Deus" echoes the prayer of the <u>malmariée</u> "En un vergier, lez une fontenelle" in her line "Bels sire doux, ja m'avez formee."

The four-line refrain in another lyric of Joao Servando takes several modes of relationship with the stanza; either the voice remains the same, or the refrain becomes indirect quotation of a second speaker, or it is independent and works as a contrapuntal voice to the whole poem, a <u>romería</u>:

> Quand'eu a San Servando
> fui un dia d'aqui
> faze-la romaria
> e meu amigu'i vi
> direi-vos con verdade
> quant'eu d'el entendi:
> > muito venho pagada,
> > por quanto lhi falei;
> > mais a m'el namorada,
> > que nunca lhi guarrei.⁶⁶

The delicacy and intricacy of the four-line refrain may be seen in a lyric of Bernal de Bonaval, "Se veess'o meu amigo." Stanza and refrain work together; speech suggested in the stanza is realized in the refrain ("lh'eu diria . . . diria-lh'eu"). Repetitions within the refrain and within the verse create a crafted double mirror effect; while verse and refrain have a patterned relationship, they each contain within themselves other inner reflections formed by the tightly worked repetitions of smaller elements. The conditional tenses and subjunctives give a dreamlike atmosphere of inner thought, and the light rhymes provide a dance-like balanced accompaniment.

Attention to refrain styles in female voice lyrics should not obscure for us the more important general observation that female voice songs are marked by binary patterns, the simple A-B movement. A discussion of the binary patterns in medieval Castilian lyric has been written by Antonio Sánchez Romeralo in the early chapters of El Villancico: estudios sobre la lírica popular en los siglos XV y XVI, and by John G. Cummins in his The Spanish Traditional Lyric. These and other critics point out the pervasive character of repetition at many levels in female voice lyric; conceptual, phonic (both at the sub-word level and at the levels of single words and groups of words and whole lines) and syntactical. To add a little more evidence to the already well-established observation about binary patterns in female voice lyric, I would like to show, in the Old French chansons de toile and the Sicilian chansons de femme, how consistently the female voice in lyric is characterized by the two-part A B pattern of rhyme.

Rhymes in Old French Chansons de Toile

A. From the Chansonnier de St. Germain-des-Prés: (anonymous songs)

```
Bele Yolanz en ses chambres seoit              aaaaBB
Oriolanz en haut solier                        aaaaaBB
En un vergier lez une fontenele                aaaaBB
Bele Doette as fenestres se siet               aaaaB
Quant vient en mai que l'on dit as lons jors   aaaaaB
Bele Yolanz en chambre koie                    aaaaBB
An halte tour se siet bele Yzabel              aaaBB
Lou samedi a soir fet la semaine               aaaBB
Bele Amelot soule an chambre feloit            aaaaBB
```

B. Songs attributed to Audefroi le Bâtard:
```
Bele Ysabiaux, pucele bien aprise              aaaBBC
Bele Ydoine se siet desous la verde olive      aaaaaBCC
An chanbre a or se siet la belle Beatris       aaaaaBB
An novel tans pascour que florist l'aube espine aaaaaBB
Bele Emmelos es pres desouz l'arbroie          aaabbB
```

C. Songs found in courtly romances:
```
Fille et mere se sient a l'orfrois             aaaB
Siet soi bele Aye as piez sa male maistre      aaaBB
La bele Doe siet au vent                       aaaaBBB
Bele Aiglentine en roial chamberine            aaaBB
Renaus et s'amie chevauche par un pre
   (one stanza fragment)                       abB
Siet soi biele Euriaus, seule est enclose      aaaabB
```

Not all stanzas are perfectly regular. In some songs of five or six stanzas some end rhymes do not conform exactly, but others in the same song do, and the majority have regularly realized A-B patterns. We see the regularity in spite of the differences of attribution to named poets or "anonymous." It does not matter whether the language is considered by critics to be "fake archaic" (Edmond Faral) or "mixed archaic and composed archaic" (Raymond Joly): in regard to the aesthetic choice of rhyme pattern the binary rhyme pattern prevails in all cases.

Binary Rhyme Patterns in Provençal and Sicilian
Female Voice Songs:

A. **Provençal**

A l'entrada del tems clar	aaaabccc
Coindeta sui	abababbb
En un vergier sotz fuella d'albespi	aaab
L'autrier 'jost una sebissa	aaab
Farai un vers pos mi sonelh	aaaBab
Ges l'Estornels	aaabccccccb
Altas ondas que venez sus la mar	aaaabb
Quan vei les pratz	ababbaba
A la fontana	aaabaac
A chantar m'er de so	aaaabab

B. **Sicilian**

Gia mai non mi conforto	ababcdcd
Rosa fresca aulentissima	aaabb
Oi lassa 'namorata	abababcdcdcd
Di dolor convien cantare	abababcccdcd

The insistence of binary A-B rhymes in the female voice lyrics is due, most probably, to the need to mark dance movements or an exchange of voices in choral singing. The chiastic ABBA pattern characteristic of male voice lyrics, on the other hand, would satisfy the need for decoration or embellishment for its own sake in the verbal texture of the poem, and for a different rhyme scheme.

As we begin to see more clearly the operation of voices in polyphonic literature, we may expect to make some changes in our critical vocabulary. In the case of lyric poetry of the newly literate Romance languages, fragments of female speech are present *to which the male voice responds* in a number of formal patterns. A male voice may construct a stanzaic poem ahead of the female voice fragment, which then acts, in the coda, as a piquant and startling finish, or the male voice can engage the female voice in a verbal duel, alternating stanzas or whole poems. It can wind a poem around the focal point of female speech or boldly juxtapose, in the opening stanza, lines of objective and reportorial "male" speech to subjective and exclamatory "female" speech. Assuming dominance, the male voice in Romance courtly lyric frames the fragmented female voice within lyrics, repertoires, and languages. When we view this process with the help of dialectical analysis, we see that "borrowed" female speech serves a crucial intention in the newly developing male voice lyric. It is not that the poet "placed this speech in the mouth of a young woman," as has so often been said, but that this speech, which belonged to women, lodged in the mind of the poet, where it became a catalyst in the formation of his own poetic style.

Notes to Chapter 2

¹ Mikhail Bakhtin, Marxism and the Philosophy of Language, p. 209.

² Chanson de toile, woman's spinning song in Old French that tells a love story in the feudal style love ethic; a military man and a love-sick girl: pastorela, a debate between a knight and a shepherdess.

³ Barbara Hernstein Smith, Poetic Closure: A Study of How Poems End (Chicago: Chicago University Press, 1968), pp. 56-70 (stanzaic forms), pp. 186-95 (the pcetic coda).

⁴ The bibliography on ḫarǧas (also transliterated as kharjas) is large. See Richard Hitchcock, The Kharjas (London: Grant and Cutler, 1977); also Samuel Miklos Stern, Arabic Strophic Poetry: Studies by Samuel Miklos Stern (Oxford: Clarendon Press, 1974).

⁵ Sola-Solé, Corpus de poesía mozárabe, pp. 97-98.

⁶ For a discussion of this treatise, see Linda Fish Compton, Andalusian Lyrical Poetry and Old Spanish Love Songs: The Muwashshah and Its Kharja (New York: New York University Press, 1976) Chapter One.

⁷ For the "pre-history" of ḫarǧa scholarship, see J. Sola-Solé, Corpus de poesía mozárabe: Las ḫarǧas andalusíes (Barcelona, 1973), 7-9.

⁸ See James T. Monroe, Hispano-Arabic Poetry: A Student Anthology (Berkeley: University of California Press, 1974) 31-32.

⁹ Raimbaut de Vaqueiras: The Poems of the Troubadour, ed. Joseph Linskill, (The Hague, 1964), pp. 98-107. English translation of the female speaker's lines in Hill and Bergin, Anthology of the Provençal Troubadours, v. 2, pp. 98--107.

¹⁰ See Marcabru's lyric in Hill and Bergin, v. 1, p. 20.

¹¹ Howard Bloch, Medieval French Literature and Law, p. 175.

¹² Bloch, p. 170.

¹³ Walter T. Pattison, The Life and Works of the Troubadour Raimbaut d'Orange (Minneapolis: University of Minneapolis Press, 1952), p. 13.

[14] Próspero Saíz, Persona and Poiesis: The Poet and the Poem in Medieval Love Lyric, p. 66.

[15] Archipreste de Hita, Libro de Buen Amor.

[16] Michel Zink, Belle, essai sur les chansons de toile, and Arthur Bernard Scharff, "The Old French 'Chansons de Toile'" (diss. Ohio State Univ., 1969).

[17] Zink, Belle, p. 80.

[18] Bruno Panvini, Le Rime della scuola siciliana, p. 231.

[19] Panvini, Le Rime, p. 534.

[20] Panvini, Le Rime, p. 495.

[21] Bartsch, Romanzen und Pastourellen, p. 137.

[22] Hans Spanke, Eine altfranzösische Leidersammlung, p. 228.

[23] Nico Van den Boogaard, Rondeaux et refrains, Bibliothèque française et romane, Series D, Vol. III Ed. George Straka, Strasbourg. (Paris: Klincksieck, 1969), p. 124.

[24] Van den Boogaard, p. 238.

[25] Le Lai d'Aristote de Henri d'Andeli, Maurice Delbouille, ed. (Paris: Société d'Edition "Les Belles Lettres," 1951).

[25] Zink, Belle, p. 85.

[27] A glimpse of fascinating biological aspects of male and female birdsong is revealed in current research. Birds must hear their species song before they are seven weeks old to be able to reproduce it. They can learn a dialect of their song, however, without having learned their species song in their own dialect. Some birds have a repertoire of a thousand songs, others sing only one. Each singer has an individual style that is recognized by his neighbors. Birds reserve aggression for members of other species after territorial rights are arranged in the annual mating period. Males are the only singers in open or moderately forested land, but in densely forested areas, female and male birds sing duets, each taking an alternate note. These birds are lifelong mates, and different pairs devise different songs. Because male and female birds have very similar genetic codes, females injected with male hormones reproduce the species song pattern almost perfectly. Researchers are currently attempting to codify features of birdsong.

[28] See the bibliography on speech and gender in Mary Ritchie Key, Male/Female Speech. (New Jersey: Scarecrow Press, 1975); and Robin Lakoff, Language and Woman's Place, (New York: Harper, 1975).

[29] Alan Deyermond, "Pero Meogo's Stags and Fountains: Symbol and Anecdote in the Traditional Lyric," Romance Philology 33 (1979) 265-283.

[30] Nunes, Cantigas d'amigo, 19.

[31] Nunes, 414.

[32] Nunes, 491.

[33] Nunes, 21.

[34] Nunes, 415.

[35] Nunes, 260.

[36] Bartsch, Rom. und Past., p. 171.

[37] Bartsch, Rom. und Past., p. 185.

[38] Bartsch, Rom. und Past., p. 306.

[39] Margit Frenk Alatorre, "Jaryas mozárabes y estribillos franceses," Nueva Revista de Filología Hispánica. 6 (1952), 281-4.

[40] Bartsch, Rom. und Past., p. 169.

[41] Bartsch, Rom. und Past., p. 25.

[42] Sola-Solé, Corpus de poesía mozárabe, p. 181.

[43] Van den Boogaard, pp. 17-25.

[44] Nunes, Cantigas d'amor, p. 66.

[45] Nunes, Cantigas d'amigo, 19.

[46] See Eugenio Asensio, Poética y realidad en el cancionero peninsular de la Edad Media (Madrid: Gredos, 1957) pp. 69-119, 177-215.

[47] J. G. Cummins, The Spanish Traditional Lyric (Oxford: Pergamon, 1977), p. 35.

[48] Cantigas de D. Joan Garcia de Guilhade, Oscar Nobiling, ed. p. 93.

[49] Nunes, 438.

50 Nunes, 476. One-word refrains are discussed by Martín de Riquer, Los Trovadores, I, p. 45.

51 Nunes, Cantigas d'amigo, vol. 2, no. 61.

52 Nunes, 62.

53 Nunes, 505.

54 Nunes, 200.

55 Nunes, 112.

56 Nunes, 60.

57 Nunes, 153.

58 Nunes, 415.

59 Nunes, 125.

60 Nunes, 347.

61 Nunes, 347.

62 Nunes, 479.

63 Nunes, 138.

64 Nunes, 379.

65 Nunes, 400.

66 Nunes, 364.

Chapter 3

> *Inferiority*: A value-bearing category that refers to the powers of the weak, countervailing against structural power, fostering continuity, creating the sentiment of the wholeness of the total community, positing the model of an undifferentiated whole whose units are whole human beings. The powers of the weak are often assigned, in hierarchic and stratified societies to females, the poor, autochthons and outcasts.
>
> Victor Turner, *Image and Pilgrimage in Medieval Society*, quoted by Elizabeth Janeway, in *Powers of the Weak*

> Two voices is the minimum for life--for existence.
>
> Mikhail Bakhtin

THE PERSONA OF THE SPEAKING WOMAN

In a polyphonic lyric style, the "other" voice (often female, "primitive," or archaic) determines the formation of lyric *structures*, because the archetypal voice (male, speaking for the newer social ethic) responds to its traditional rhythms and rhymes by amalgamation or contrast as it surrounds and overtakes it (Chapter 2). The *thematic relationship* of the two voices, however, proceeds in a different direction, and we must approach it from the opposite perspective. Here, conversely, the host voice controls the semantic interpretation of "borrowed" or reported speech. The imperative ideological need of the dominant voice assigns cultural value to the secondary or complementary voice. The male troubadour in courtly lyric, then, presents the female speaker in many different locally-determined guises which create, nevertheless, a single male/female voice dialectic. The *persona* of the speaking woman, in the important role of minority voice, complements the male speaker from her position of cultural inferiority. The present chapter will examine in detail the *personae* of the female speakers in the Romance literatures of our study: Mozarabic Spanish, Galician-Portuguese, Provençal, Old French, and Italian. Chapter four (Part II of the study of *persona*) will place the female voice within its cultural context. Here we will find, notwithstanding differences of local characterization, a unity of semiotic function in its relation to the archetypal male voice.

When we consider the differences in the female voice in the individual Romance languages, we will be dealing with the poems on the level of the concrete: specific situations, themes, and physical descriptions, both by the male narrator and by the female speaker herself. These descriptions and situations arise out of the surface appearances of the local society for which the songs serve as a source of social information. When we consider the unifying features of the female *persona*, we will look at some relations of the male and female voice which are more symbolic and cross-cultural: language use, economic position, social attitude, and the female speaker's rhetoric of ethos, logos, or pathos. Both perspectives are necessary for a full understanding of our subject (and they are by no means entirely separable) but we should not permit the first view, of differences in surface features, to obscure our clear view of the underlying unity in the female speaker's *persona* throughout Romance courtly lyric at the moment of its entry into written literature. As we will see in Chapter 4, only by means of the dialectical analysis of the female voice in the courtly lyric style of one language area will we be able to approach larger and more universal questions about the female voice in lyric poetry of other times and places.

The speaker of the Mozarabic Spanish women's songs is a young, unmarried woman (the age of thirteen is mentioned in one lyric, harǧa 7b), who is passionately in love.[1] The poet/narrator describes her as a slim-waisted and beautiful girl who sings in the night to cure his love-sickness (52, 4, 27). She speaks a foreign, Christian language (35, 45, 40a), and she has a beautiful voice (50, 47). He tells us that she is "terrorized at the departure of her lover" (35), and she is driven mad by his absence (5a, 26, 43). In one song she is on the seashore lamenting as her lover is leaving (10). She is often said to be in a state of hopeless desperation and may have "no other hope than to go to him" (11, 13). She may be a virgin who wants the hated guardian to disappear (47), or simply feel fear of the guardian (3). One of the singers was seduced by a lover who now makes her sick with his scorn and disdain (23). A scene of violence is described by one poet/narrator, "When I caught her alone . . . and was tearing her garments off with force, she sang to her mother with disdain . . ." (49). In another description, she is "full of passion . . . and did not cease complaining of one who was unjust toward her" (11). She may be "a young woman full of bitterness, crying like one whose lover has gone away" (42). The motif of sleeplessness is brought into the introduction of the young singer (44).

The characteristics of the female singer given by the poet/narrator in the fifth stanza of the *muwashsha* often are, as we found in Chapter two, an *amplification* of the woman's song itself. When we hear the words of the short and passionate lyric, we recognize the themes contained in the poet's introduction: dying for love, lament for the absent lover, fear of the guardian, the indelicate lover, praise of the beloved's beauty. She often addresses her song to the mother, to whom she turns for comfort and support:

> Oh, my dearest mother, tomorrow I will see the handsome Abu'l 'Haggag who shines like the dawn (25a)

> This shameless man, mother, this madman attacks me with force, and we are lost in his ocean wave (49)

and a brief exclamation,

> What shall I do, mother, my lover is at the door? (39)

But she may also address her girlfriends:

> Tell me, friends, how to stop my sickness. I cannot live without my lover and will go to find him. (33)

or her whole family:

> Come, all my people! I want the arrow; my lover is singing in Valencia to someone else. (19)

She often calls to her lover directly:

> Oh, my seducer, come here when
> the tasks of war release you. (46)

> Mouth of pearls, sweet as honey,
> Kiss me
> Come to me, lover, to make love,
> As we did the other day. (43)

She may make erotic suggestions to him:

> You will not see me except on condition
> That you join my ankle bracelets to my earrings. (48)

She mentions her clothing; she will go to a festival on St. John's Day and wear a brocade dress (24) and will wear the costume of a merchant in disguise when she goes to seek her lover in Sevilla (20). In another lyric (36) she says that her beauty is her clothing; her unadorned white neck is what her lover wants so she does not wish for a pearl necklace.

The expressive characteristics of the Mozarabic Spanish lyrics, as we can see, are brevity, intensity, and narrow thematic focus. The motifs of the call to the lover, the indelicate lover, confidence to a mother, seeking the lover in the night or in a faraway place, and sleeplessness are characteristics of women's songs in archaic and Hellenistic Greek lyric poetry. In a comparative study, "Poesía griega 'De Amigo' y poesía arábigo-española," the classicist Elvira Gangutia Elícegui traces similar themes in women's songs through the history of Mediterranean lyric poetry.[2] She proposes the concept of a regional formation of women's lyrics beginning in early Sumerian, Egyptian and Syrian cult worship of Aphrodite/Adonis and other gods. Women's songs were spread to towns and villages around the shores of the Mediterranean by Greek colonists and traders during the Hellenistic expansion. In Northern Africa and Spain, the ancient cultic and ritual literature would survive in oral tradition through changes in religions and empires to play an important role in the shaping of Romance lyric. In other studies of the Mozarabic Spanish lyric, Margit Frenk Alatorre underlines the folkloric, "pre-literary," nature of the ḫarǧa and its narrow range of styles.[3] In this corpus, we do not find discussion of events, but only a vivid personal cri du coeur. We do not find dance songs, dialogues, debates, or common Romance forms such as the pastorela and malmariée songs. We do find brilliant and compressed lyrics that express feelings from adoration of the lover to outspoken and daring sexual references, all in a deliberately unsophisticated patois.

The large majority of the over five hundred women's songs in the Galician-Portuguese corpus are social and chatty in tone. Girls in love talk to their boyfriends, their mothers, and their girlfriends. Mothers talk to daughters. The theme of these lyrics is the ordeal of parting: the departure, absence, and return of the lover in an anxious world of uncertain relationships.[4] The variety and fascination of the lyrics lie in the many attitudes the girl, with her mother and her companions, explores in regard to her situation. Her love is the constant element. The changes, and the interest in the lyrics, come from her deliberations about a possible course of action. Her rhetoric in lyric after lyric is interrogative. Shall she give him permission to leave? Did he leave without her permission? If he did, will she take him back? Why did he go?

> Porque se foi d'aqui meu amigo
> sen meu mandad'e non mi'o fez saber,
> quand'el veer por falar comigo,
> assanhar-m'ei e farei-lh'entender
> que outra vez non se vaia d'aqui
> per nulha ren sen mandado de mi.[5]
> (Nunes 219)

> Fostes-vos vós, meu amigo, d'aqui
> sen meu mandad'e nulha ren falar
> mi non quisestes, mais oj'ao entrar,
> se por mesura non fosse de mi,
> > me vos eu vira, non mi venha ben
> > nunca de Deus, nen donde m'oje ven.
> > (Nunes 458)

The girl suffers greatly in the lover's absence or disloyalty:

> Ai madre, nunca mal sentiu,
> nen soubi que x'era pesar
> a que seu amigo non viu,
> com'oj'eu vi o meu, falar
> > con outra, mais, poi-lo eu vi,
> > con pesar ouvi a morrer i.
> > (Nunes 403)

> Quando se foi noutro dia d'aqui
> o meu amigo, roguei-lh'eu por Deus,
> chorando muito destes olhos meus,
> que non tardass'e disse-m'el assi:
> > que nunca Deus lhi desse de mi ben,
> > se non veesse mui ced', e non ven.
> > (Nunes 99)

The etiquette of mother-daughter-lover relations is explored in many songs:

> Preguntar-vos quer'eu madre,
> que me digades verdade:
> > se ousará meu amigo
> > ante vós falar comigo. (Nunes 417)

and the mother often sings to her daughter, as in this <u>barcarola</u>:

> El-rei de Portugale
> barcas mandou lavrare
> > e lá irá nas barcas migo,
> > mia filha, o voss'amigo.   (Nunes 384)

The theme of a trip to a religious shrine to find the lover often involves a request for permission from the mother:

> Treides, ai mia madr', en romaria
> orar u chamam Santa Cecilia:
> > e, louçana irei,
> ca já i est'o que namorei,
> > e, louçana, irei.   (Nunes 485)

Over a dozen lyrics are distinctly poems of mutual love, in which the woman is not in conflict with her lover, but full of joy, as in this lovely poem of King Dinis:

> Pois que diz meu amigo
> que se quer ir comigo,
> [e], pois que a el praz,
> praz a mi, ben vos digo;
> est' é o meu solaz.   (Nunes 51)

The theme of shared happiness in love, present in the <u>cantigas de amigo</u>, is found throughout medieval Romance lyric, but it has been seldom studied or commented.

Because of their extreme interest and beauty, the lyrics with nature symbolism of fountains, animals and pine trees have been often anthologized and commented. Poems of the type:

> Enas verdes ervas
> vi anda-las cervas
> meu amigo.
>
> Enos verdes prados
> vi los cervos bravos,
> meu amigo.   (Nunes 416)

form a distinct thematic sub-group within the <u>cantigas de amigo</u>, whose motifs may be found in Biblical or even earlier Indo-European folklore, as Alan Deyermond has shown.[6] Only a few poets have songs of this type in their repertoires, although the entire corpus (eight songs only) of Martim Codax consists of "nature" songs; the majority have none at all.

For the most part, the <u>cantigas de amigo</u> concern the power balance between the woman who stays at home and laments her absent lover, plots to get him back, declares her position in regard to his requests, while talking over the pros and cons of her situation with her mother, lover and girlfriend. The mother may like the young man and encourage her daughter, even pointing him out the next time she sees him. Frequently the mother disapproves, and beatings are mentioned. A mother tells her daughter to dress well to catch a man. In dialogues with the "amigo" he often pleads, she says no, or, occasionally, yes. He wants to leave, how much does he love her? How can he leave and cause her pain? She may tell her girlfriends that both she and her friend are too frightened to speak. In one lyric she tells a shy man to leave; she has no time for a man who cannot talk. In another she tells her boyfriend that they should enjoy love, and not suffer from it, but be open with each other. She may also discuss her girlfriend's love affair with her <u>amigo</u>, and ask for his advice.

In a view now considered anachronistic, critics have called the female speaker of Galician-Portuguese <u>cantigas de amigo</u> a bourgeoise, because the supposed chaste moral tones and domestic scenes reveal the song's middle class origin. Another view is that the women's songs in Galician-Portuguese are entirely the creation of the court poet's imagination, and are little different from the men's love songs. To describe the <u>cantigas de amigo</u> uniformly as "declarations of love" as C. P. Bagley does is to ignore their thematic variety and social content.[7] So much detailed attention to the problem of separation has the sound of a concern for a serious social problem. One can make comparisons with tenth and eleventh-century Japanese middle-class Heian women's poetry, or Tamil court poetry of the second and third centuries, where a scenario of stock characters (mother, girl, boyfriend, girlfriend) discuss their social relationships with vivid exactness. The poets of medieval Portugal have used the theme of womanly deliberation on the social consequences of young men leaving the matrilocal situation for a distant court or war.

The <u>persona</u> of the speaking woman in Provençal lyric is complex and fascinating. In anonymous dance songs, <u>albas</u>, and love lyrics, she shows great self-confidence and personal power. She is the verbal equal or superior of the male speaker in the dialogues. She seeks rational explanations for any unhappiness she feels, blaming unacceptable behavior frankly and candidly. Yet, along with the positive, self-affirming linguistic portrait, we find also that the male troubadour has strongly marked the female speaker as inferior in economic and social position. Because of this thematic marking, her voice continues to function as a carrier of heterodox values.

For this investigation, I have chosen a corpus of thirty-six lyrics in which a woman is the principal or an equal speaker.[8] The songs might be arranged in various ways: by chronology, authorship, or type (<u>canso</u>, <u>tenso</u>, <u>pastorela</u>); however, the most logical division is into five thematic categories: joyful love songs, laments, dance songs, light parodies, and burlesques (low comedy and fable). Significantly, the first two and the last two categories present a reverse image of each other; love, exalted in the first group, is deflated by parody; passionate love-longing finds a counterpart in cool comments from levelheaded <u>tozas</u>. The general division of the songs, then, into serious and comic reflects the division of all Provençal lyric into its balance of <u>canso</u> and <u>sirventès</u>.

In the category which I have designated as "joyful love songs," we hear the voice of frank, unrepentant desire, with an expectancy of fulfillment in love, both physical and spiritual. In spite of the fact that Provençal women lived in a Christian culture whose official dogma glorified virginity and condemned female sexuality, the woman's voice as we hear it in song gives open-hearted expression to <u>ioi</u> in love relationships, without any sense of Christian guilt.[9] The theme of joyful love begins with the earliest appearance of a woman speaker in Provençal literature, in the bilingual <u>alba</u> (Latin-Provençal) "Phebi claro nondum orto iubare." The theme continues in the anonymous dance song "A l'entrade del tens clar--eya," with its folkloric Queen of April (<u>la regine avrillouse</u>) through the twelfth century into the work of the last troubadours to write in Provençal, Giraut Riquier and Cerverí de Girona at the end of the thirteenth century. Whenever it appears in Provençal, the woman's voice is self-assured and confident of her power. She asks for love. and supports her right to ask by a reasoned theory of love based on equality in love relationships. She uses humor and wit to defend her position, states her demands in clear and unmistakable terms, but is willing to be persuaded when her lover shows that he can meet her requirements. She speaks with a voice of authority, a kind of authority that sustains and supports a social order based on fearless relations between women and men.

> Fin ioi me don' alegranssa
> per qu'eu chan plus gaimen
> e no m'o teing a pensanssa[10]

sings the Comtessa de Dia, and she takes pleasure in the expression of happiness:

> ab ioi et ab joven m'apais
> et ioi e iovens m'apaia[11]

Her wit is typical Provençal word-play: she uses grammatical endrhymes for her theme of the happiness of a woman in love. Thus speaks Na Tibors on a woman's feelings of desire:

> Bels dous amics, ben vos posc en ver dir
> Que anc no fo qu'ieu estes ses desir
> per vos . . .
> Ni anc no fo sazons que m'en pentis.[12]

The woman of the beautiful anonymous <u>canso</u> "Quan vei los praz verdesir" sings to her lover in these words:

> A deus, com serai garida
> s'aissi devengues
> una noit per escarida
> qu'a me s'en vengues . . ..[13]

The above passages are from <u>cansos</u> which betray no trace of the interpretation of a courtly love ethic as tormented love ennobled by humble service to a distant, imperious lover. On the contrary, love here is valued when it is fulfilled. Her sense of joy is even increased by the local gossips, the lauzengiers, as we see in this bold challenge:

>   e lor malsdiz non m'esglaia
>   anz en son dos tanz plus gais.[14]

Thus, not only does the woman's voice show consciousness of her desire for love, but it shows a conception of love that requires mutual caring and equality of emotional response in each partner.

    A significant group of love songs expressing the theme of mutual love exists in Provençal lyric, as well as in the secular lyric of other medieval vernacular languages, and this theme has never been given the critical attention it deserves. The songs "L'Autre dia" of Gavaudan, and "L'Autrier cavalgada" of Gui d'Ussel illustrate the "mutuality" love ethic. The latter poem is a model of reciprocity in its use of direct discourse. Like the knight, the shepherdess is a singer, and a line of her song is given, "Lassa, mal viu qui pert son jauzimen." The knight and <u>pastora</u> tell each other their stories of rejection by past lovers, and each one's comprehension of the other's experience is made explicit by repetitions:

>   he: com a vos a fag
>   aquel que us oblida
>   she: trobas del forfag
>   que us a fag tan lag.[15]

Further repetitions of an entire line, "si·m n'es acort" indicate that each partner recognizes the other's right of assent.

    Gavaudan's "L'Autre dia" shows the lovers' concern for justifying their passion. He feels that God must have arranged this happy meeting. She agrees, moving quickly to tell her desire:

>   Senher, oc, quar nos ajustet
>   Qu'alre no vuilh ni queria
>   E, si us platz, a mi plairia
>   So don hom plus me castiet . . . .[16]

He makes another appeal to God, and concludes that they are both free to abandon themselves to their passion, "Vostre merce e la mia / Yssit em d'autre baylia." In this charming poem, the lover appeals to God for success in his love affair. The sense that God does not frown on sexual love, indeed, lends assistance to lovers, finds its clearest expression, perhaps, in the <u>alba</u> "Reis glorious, verais lums e clartatz" of Guiraut de Bornelh, in which Christ is the divine accomplice to a night of adulterous love--although it is a common element in the courtly poetry of France.

The equation of harmony, musical sound, and mutual love is praised by Jaufre Rudel in the <u>canso</u> "Pro ai del chan essenhadors." The first strophe gives praise to the sweet sounds of the soft season, although the comfort of love is the best of these harmonies. Then, in the next stanza, the quality of mutual love is given brilliant linguistic form in the phrase "jauzens jauzitz,"

> Las pimpas sian als pastors
> Et als enfans burdens petitz
> E mias sion tals amors
> Don ieu sia jauzens jauzitz.[17]

The worth of her lover's character forms a large part of the Provençal woman speaker's concern as we hear it in song. Her independence of judgment about him is evident in many songs. The Comtessa de Dia couches her thought in word-play:

> Mout me plai car sai que val mais
> sel qu'ieu plus desir que m'aia[18]

while Castelloza speaks directly:

> Amics, s'ie us trobes avinen
> Humil e franc e de bona merce
> Be us amera . . . [19]

Garsende de Sabran adds guidance to judgment:

> Vos que·m semblatz dels corals amadors
> Ja no volgra que fossetz tan doptanz[20]

"Lady H," in a tenso with "Rofin" admires and requests forceful, spontaneous behavior in a passionate lover:

> A fin amic non tol paors
> Rofin, de penre jauzimens . . .
> Qu'ab jazer et ab remirar
> L'amors corals recaliva
> Tant fort que non au ni non ve
> Ni conois quan fai mal o be.[21]

A "Good Lady" tells her <u>donzela</u> exact reasons for her displeasure:

> Na donzela, be·m deu esser salvatge
> quan el gaba ni se vana de me
> tan a son cor fol e leu e volatge
> que m'amistat en lunha re no's te,[22]

and she sets conditions for a relationship:

> --Si m'amor vol, na donzela, que renda
> ben li er ops que sia gais e pros,
> francs e umils, qu'ab nulh om no·s contenda
> qu'a me non tanh om fel ni ergulhos.[23]

One final example of the woman's voice exercising independent, articulate opinion about the love relation comes from the anonymous tenso, "Amics, en gran cossirier" (which has been attributed both to La Comtessa de Dia and to Raimbaut d'Aurenga):

> donecx, per que us metetz amaire
> pus a me laissatz tot lo mal?
> quar abduy no·l partem egual.[24]

Such a plethora of examples should help, I believe, to counteract the mistaken conception that the Provençal woman's voice is a direct imitation of the male poet's, and has no alternative love ethic. We find theoretical support for the "mutuality" ethic stated by Maria de Ventadorn in a tenso with Gui d'Ussel. After agreeing with Gui's statement on equal relations in friendship, "Qu'en dos amics no deu aver major," she adds her own formulation:

> Gui, tot so don es cobeitos
> deu drutz ab merce demandar
> e dompna pot o comandar
> e deu ben pregar a sazos--
> E·l dompna deu a son drut far honor
> cum ad amic, mas non com a seignor.[25]

Maria asserts both the rights of the male lover to ask for what he wants, and the lady's right to deal with his request as she wishes, while specifically rejecting the hierarchical relation between lovers ("Mas non com a seignor") in favor of the mutuality of friendship.

Alamanda was not a noble lady as was Maria de Ventadorn. but a lady's donzela: nevertheless, she has her ideas clearly in mind when she acts as advisor to Guiraut de Bornelh in the tenso, "S'ie us quier conseill, bell'ami 'Alamanda." She gives each partner responsibility in case of an offense. and counsels patient effort and caressing words to prevent a discord from spreading:

> Car si·l'us falh, l'alre conve que blanda
> que lor destrics no crescha ni s'espanda[26]

Techniques of reconciliation are naturally a part of a mutual love ethic.

To sum up this first group of songs, then, we can say that a theme of joyful love emerges clearly articulated in the woman's voice. Perhaps because women did not see themselves as they were defined by Christian dogma into a dichotomy of "virgin/whore," they speak in song from a point of view that takes both partners as subjects, love being something that happens to both of them. Their typical description of love is <u>not</u> pain willingly suffered, and they actively search for and try to cure the cause of pain. The pride of tortured hearts, which quickly turns to general condemnation, is absent, as it is present in these lines of Bernart de Ventadorn's "Can la frej' aura venta":

> Si d'aisso m essertana,
> d'autra vetz la·n creirai
> o si que no, ja mai
> no creirai crestiana. [27]

The woman's voice, on the contrary, states that love, to be joyful, must be a reciprocal, shared experience. When a problem exists in the relationship, the explanation is sought not in the "nature of man," but in specific behavior which prevents mutual happiness.

Critical opinion, however, has hardly begun to explore the theme of mutual love in Provençal lyric. Joan Ferrante dismisses the Provençal women poets with a sentence, "The Provençal women who wrote lyric poetry are not mentioned because they employ the same conventions as the men.[28] This statement cannot be based on a fresh study of the lyrics they wrote. A more balanced approach to the general subject is found in John Moore's <u>Love in 12th Century France</u>. Moore writes, "The love songs of the troubadours present no well-defined set of ideas which can be neatly labeled "courtly love." They contain, rather, a spectrum of attitudes.[29] The theme of mutual love exists not only in the women's voice in Provençal, but in other medieval secular lyrics in Galician-Portuguese, as we have seen.[30]

When we turn to the second group of songs, the songs of loss, we find a voice that differs from its Greek and Hispano-Arabic equivalent by a tone that is less desperate and more self-conscious. Within the beautiful and haunting laments, we find the Provençal woman seeking reasons and explanations for the loss of love. Her voice reveals her self-awareness; she wants to know a specific cause for her experience. The lament "A chantar m'er" of la Comtessa de Dia shows the woman pursuing her need to understand in detail; is he acting from pride or from ill-will?

> Ieu vuoill saber, lo mieus bels amics gens
> Perque vos m'etz tant fers ni tant salvatges,
> No sai si s'es orguoills o maltalens.[31]

Azalais de Porcairages and Clara d'Anduza wrote laments in which the woman speaker gives an explanation for her unhappy state. In the former's "Ar em al freg temps vengut," the mistake was to choose a man of wealth and power. She knows he loves her, but he is too far away:

> Domna met mot mal s'amor
> Que ab ric hom plaideia . . .[32]

The woman of Clara d'Anduza's song "En greu esmai et en greu pessamen" blames <u>lauzengiers</u> for her lover's absence. In rebellion against convention, she protests that frustration will not ennoble her spirit:

> Cel que.m blasma vostr'amor ni.m defen
> No podon far en re mon cor melhor,

and she regrets her marital helplessness, since anger decreases her creativity in composing songs:

> Amics, tan ai d'ira e de feunia
> Quar no vos vei, que quant ieu cug cantar
> Plang e sospir; perqu'ieu no posc so far
> A mas coblas que l cors complir volria.[33]

Anna Granville Hatcher has described another song of loss, Marcabru's "A la fontana del vergier."[34] The female speaker blames successively Jesus, King Louis, and God for her lover's absence. The last line of the lyric carries the sequence of blame to its logical limit; the man who left her must not have thought much of her:

> . . . mas pauc mi tey
> Que trop s'es de mi alonhatz[35]

Independence of mind, feelings of self-worth, and interest in particular details mark this woman's voice as typical in Provençal lyric. She expresses heterodox, even subversive thoughts in her genuine self-centeredness.

Two further laments illustrate the rationalizing tendency even in the songs of loss. The lady of "Quan vei les praz verdesir" advises and reflects "Domna que amors aten / ben deu aver fin coratge." and she cautions "Domna qui amic no a / ben si gart que mais non aja."[36] These <u>sententiae</u> are especially remarkable because they are set in a song of strong emotional tone established by a refrain. "Aei," and archaic diction marked by parallelism. If we compare the lament "Altas ondas que venez sus la mar" of

Raimbaut de Vaqueiras to "Ondas do mar de Vigo," a poem of the Galician-Portuguese poet Martin Codax, we see the change to a distinctly rationalizing tone in Provençal. Whereas all three stanzas of Martin Codax' song repeat a similar pattern of address to waves followed by an exclamation,

> Ondas do mar de Vigo
> Se vistes meu amigo?
> E ai Deus, se verra cedo![37]

the Provençal speaker addresses the world at large and her own conscience, as well as the waves. A Latinate syntax "car . . . " "e . . . e" increases the sense of reasoning about experience:

> Mal amar fai vassal d'estran pais
> car en plor tornan e sos jocs e sos ris.[38]

We see, then, in the songs of lament and complaint, a selfconscious, rationalizing voice added to the expression of emotion. This is true even in the traditional forms least hospitable to analytic statement. The Provençal woman in love does not relish the pain of sadness, or think of sorrow as a source of perfection; indeed, the idea is consciously rejected. She considers herself worthy of love and explores her experience with a factual, realistic mind even while she laments the pain of loss.

The dance songs of the third group are among the most fascinating of all medieval lyrics. They present a woman's emotional world that is sharply divided inro two poles; attraction for a young lover and hostility toward an old husband, the gilos, or "jealous one." The subject of the song, a young woman, is given flattering epithets; she is delgada, coindeta, savorouse. She characterizes herself as creative, a joyful maker of songs and dances, who wants to be happy. Her impulses toward the husband range from a mild desire to irritate him:

> A l'entrade del tens clar--eya
>
> pir ioie recomencar--eya
> e pir ialous irritar--eya
> vol la regine mostrar
>
> > k'ele est si amourouse[39]

to murderous thoughts:

> Coindeta sui, si cum n'ai greu cossire
> per mon marit, quar ne'l voil ne•l desire
> anz, quant lo vei, ne son tanr vergoignosa
> qu'eu prec la mort que•l venga tost aucire.[40]

He, on the other hand, may be simply an interference in the woman's dance:

> Lo reis i vent d'autre part--eya
> pir la dance destorbar--eya
> que il est en cremetar--eya
> que on ne li vuelle emblar
> la regine avrillouse
> a la vi', a la vie, ialous!
> lassaz nos, lassaz nos
> ballar entre nos, entre nos

or a physical danger when he beats her with a club,

> Se·l gilos mi menazza
> de baston ni de mazza
> del batre si se·l faza . . .[41]

The consistent emotional duality in the dance songs has caused much critical comment.[42] Peter Dronke brings out their dramatic quality, and suggests that they are remainders of Greek-inspired agricultural and fertility rituals, and the worship of Aphrodite. Willard Trask sees in them evidence of indigenous lyric poetries of the pre-literate European societies.[43] A return to the question of origins, however, does not provide an explanation for their survival in thirteenth-century Provençal culture. We still lack an adequate theory to help us understand what Jeanroy called their "grâce mutine et folâtre," the gleeful, almost inhuman way in which the male characters in the woman's mind are divided into distinctly opposite categories of bad and good.[44] Some new thoughts on this theme can be found in the current research in women's studies and ethnomusicology.

In her article, "The Female World of Love and Ritual," Carroll Smith-Rosenberg documents eighteenth and nineteenth-century "support networks" in which women who had only formal contact with the man's world formed close and loving relationships within an all-female world.[45] Especially pertinent to the themes of this section of dance songs is her research on courtship and marriage attitudes. Young women, although wanting and seeking the advantages of marriage, made fun of their suitors and harassed them when they could. In marriage, rigid gender role differentiation brought in its train emotional segregation. Women held husbands at an emotional distance, while cherishing female members of their support group. Within the physically and emotionally intimate world of female friendships, women developed their sense of inner security and self-esteem.

The role of songs in the daily life of the woman's group in pre-literate societies has been studied by Sophie Drinker.[46] She shows that women typically take charge of the birth, puberty, marriage, and death ceremonies in their villages. Although twentieth-century urban American women are out of touch with this pattern, women historically have used song at rituals surrounding the major life events. Music literally accompanied women from the cradle to the grave. Songs fulfilled women's need for diversion at work, and guidance and comfort in their social roles. More than a verbal teaching, music initiated women into the rhythms and attitudes that their cultural group expected them to adopt. In this, the woman's song met the same need as the male epic. In the case of the Provençal dance songs, their function may well have been to assist a young woman to come to terms with a truly ambiguous life situation: her healthy and normal desire for an attractive sexual partner in conflict with a marriage choice beyond her control. Marriage itself was desirable, since only through marriage could she advance in social status and personal power. The dance, then, with its strong rhythmic compulsion and affirmation of her desirable qualities (coindeta, delgada, savorouse) compelled acceptance of this situation and was joyful. The dual attitude toward men, attraction and repulsion, showed women that the conflict of their emotional attachments was socially legitimized. A woman thus avoided alternatives of rebellion, isolation, or madness. Her fragmented emotions were expressed openly in group music, so that she could feel them as whole and bear them. She was enabled to face with courage and even gaiety the dangers and brutality that were associated with home warfare and childbirth. In a society whose official religion had no place for the sexual woman, the dance songs functioned as a retreat from an impossible contradiction. In this sense they were pre-Christian or anti-Christian, allowing women expressions of self-confidence and joy.

Our first example of songs of satire (the fourth thematic group) is a _tenso_ on marriage. Lady Alaisna and Lady Iselda ask their friend Lady Carenza for advice on the question of whether it is better to take a husband or remain a virgin. Not to marry seems too hard, but marriage brings sagging breasts and a bothersome belly:

> que las tetinhas pendon aval jos
> e'l ventrilhs es cargatz e enojos.[47]

Both the religious and secular alternatives are explored frankly in an affectionate but clear-sighted discourse.

The popularity of songs of satire, especially the _pastorela_, indicates that the courtly audience enjoyed laughing at its pretensions. The plot line of the _pastorela_ remained remarkably stable through one hundred and fifty years of Provençal lyric. A knight riding in the country hears or sees a young shepherdess who is often singing some lines that are quoted. He compliments, and she retorts with a sharptongued sally. A "he said-she said" patter is set up, in which he always makes an offer, and she gives a quick-witted reply. This dramatic formula mocks the courtly situation while providing a compliment for both sexes. Men who were facing witty women in real life could empathize with a knight trying dozens of schemes to get past the woman's armor of wit. But behind his usually ineffectual attempts at sex, the knight is a constant fountain of eagerness, so that male listeners could identify with the ever-willing knight full of sap. Female listeners, although pictured as socially inferior, could see themselves as <u>avenante</u>, and carriers of the highly valued quality of <u>mezura</u>.

The place and provenance of the medieval <u>pastorela</u> has a long history in critical literature.[48] Between the conflicting claims of Greek and Latin origin, a reconciling view would relate the Latin to the Greek in a popular comedy form of <u>satura</u>, and distinguish it from satire, which Dryden called "the defamation of others." <u>Satura</u> is a medley of folk comedy, with character sketches presented in dramatic form verging on caricature. In his article "Satura and Satire," R. J. Tiddy describes <u>satura</u> as "discursive, mild and hospitable, with prudential maxims, simple jokes, and a free range of subject.[49] This form passed from Greek to Latin through the first known writer of <u>satura</u> in Latin, Ennius, who was born in 239 B.C. in a bilingual town where Oscan and Greek and perhaps very little Latin were spoken. Ennius adapted Greek forms, meters, and mythology to the Latin language. Lucilius, Varro, and Horace also wrote <u>satura</u>. Of Greek influence on Varro, Tiddy writes:

> Varro's humorous sympathy was native to him and perhaps native to <u>satura</u>. But even in this Greek influence can be traced. According to Cicero he followed Menippus of Gadara, and Menippus no doubt helped to keep Varro's satire sweet upon his tongue . . . This was the sunny way of Greek satire, and it was wholesome for Roman satire.[50]

The distinction between humorous folk comedy and bitter personal and political satire marks Provençal lyric. The woman's voice in the <u>pastorela</u> belongs to the Greek-inspired light and sunny humor that keeps us laughing while it makes fun of the sexual game.

Comic songs that penetrate to a deeper level of humor are those that burlesque the ridiculous aspects of sexuality; verbal deceit and misplaced desire. They differ from the light-hearted wit of the <u>pastorela</u> in their use of darker motifs. Here we find strange language, folkloric and symbolic devices, and wilder narrative. Each song of this group contains distorted language. The mute of William IX's

"Farai un vers pos mi sonelh" can only utter "barbariol, barbariol, barbarian" and his lack of speech signals freedom from public disclosure to the women who are eager to indulge with him.[51] In the bird songs of Marcabru and Peire d'Alvernhe the <u>estornel</u> and <u>rossinhol</u> speak freely with the lady and she with the bird. Marcabru's 'starling' poem "Ges l'estornels non s'oblida" is much stronger than the "Ben a tengut dreg viatge" of Peire d'Alvernhe. In both songs the lady and bird converse, but in the earlier poem the lady's language is more direct; she is willing to play without commitment since her sworn lover is away:

> La cambr'er de cel guarnida,
> D'un ric jauzir per jauzida,
> C'ab dous baisar s'es sentida
> Desotz se plat de plazensa.
> > Vai e di
> > Qu'el mati
> > Si·aisi,
> > Que sotz pi
> > Farem fi,
> > Sotz lui mi,
> D'esta malvolensa. [52]

The honest realism of the woman who knows she does not love the man, but is happy to share physical pleasure contrasts with the moralism of the lady of the later poem by Peire d'Alvernhe. That lady gives an assurance of her love, but no meeting place, and a little sermon on <u>bon' amors e amistatz</u>. The bird, symbol of the soul and intermediary between heaven and earth, associates love and death: the <u>estornel</u> by the color black, and the <u>rossinhol</u> by singing at night. The folkloric elements express imaginatively the unreal quality of love at a distance, the disparity between lover and love object.

The lady of Raimbaut de Vaqueiras' "Domna, tant vos ai pregada" uses incomprehensible speech--castigating her Provençal suppliant in a foreign language as though the message and its form were indivisible. He cannot "hear" such abusive thoughts. Likewise, perceptual disorientation begins from the first line of William IX's "Farai un vers pos mi sonelh," a lusty fabliau. The narrator is asleep standing in the sun; the story may be a dream. Food and nudity are both here, motifs typical of medieval jest. I cannot find a specifically brown red cat in symbol books, but the cat itself is a symbol of crafty triumph over enemies; all the more ironic here, then, since he triumphs despite <u>their</u> cat. The numerology is an interesting detail; 100 and 8 are first mentioned separately, the mute remaining eight days receiving one hundred scratches, and the the numbers are combined, 188 being the number of his sexual acts, as though scratches and days added up.

A thematic study of the female <u>persona</u> in a group of
Provençal secular lyrics reveals a heterodox, anti-Christian
attitude about male-female love relations that is nevertheless quite different from the hierarchical male courtly love
ethic. In the love songs, we have seen a "mutual love"
ethic whose requirement is an egalitarian division of power
between the lovers. In the laments, we have seen a rationalizing tone consistent with the characteristic self-aware
attitude of the female <u>persona</u> in Provençal lyric. Indeed,
the Provençal woman seeks an explanation for her experience
even in the most emotional songs of love loss. The dance
songs were considered from a cultural point of view, as a
means of adjustment to the ambiguity of the marriage situation. The song legitimates emotional conflict in a major
area of life, thus fulfilling a vital social need. The
archaic form of contrasting opposites, life/death, survived
from pagan ritual, not because anyone worshipped Persephone/
Demeter, but because the form of the song suited the contemporary cultural situation for women. Finally, the rich
comic treatment of sexual mores should not surprise us in a
literature that shines with brilliant and caustic humor.
The comic songs provide the quintessential quality of Provençal art; the play of strong contrasts, in sound, rhythm,
and theme. The themes include, for the woman's voice,
mutual happiness in love, reasoned understanding of the
experience of loss, self-defense by wit, and outrageous
orgy. The woman's voice in Provençal lyric belongs both to
a pre-Christian Mediterranean tradition and to its own time.

Audacious speech in the female <u>persona</u> caught the attention of French critics from the start of modern medieval
studies; not only refrains with uninhibited exclamations:

>   Au cuer les ai, les jolis malz
>   Coment an guariroie?

and

>   Les mamelettes me poignent
>   Je ferai novel ami,

but also apparent rebellion against Church and marriage:

>   Je sant les douls mals leis ma centurete,
>   malois soit de Deu ki me fist nonnete!

and

>   Soufrés, maris, et si ne vos anuit
>   Demain m'arés et mes amis anuit[53]

that Jeanroy called "mutine et folâtre" and incomprehensible
if they were to be taken seriously. Such songs point to a
pre-literary stratum of oral lyric, "pre-courtly" in its

unrestrained expression and feminine in voice. With the
discovery in the 1940's of further examples of <u>chansons de
femme</u> as the earliest specimens of Romance lyric, the Mozarabic <u>ḫarǧas</u>, the theory of a traditional women's song
style surviving into written, courtly lyric gained new
credibility. Comparative studies in the 1950's and 1960's
by Pierre Le Gentil, Leo Spitzer, Peter Dronke and others
linked the strands of women's songs in early Romance and
German lyric.[54] A separate, pre-courtly female voice
became a strong critical position. More recent studies, and
collections of texts, on the Old French refrain (by Nico van
den Boogaard), on the <u>pastourelle</u> and <u>chanson de toile</u> (by
Michel Zink) and on a typology of genres (by Pierre Bec)
have clarified many aspects of the French woman's song. The
work on French medieval poetics of Edmond Faral and Paul
Zumthor has contributed indispensible formulations to the
special studies concerning the French <u>chansons de femme</u>. It
is on the firm foundation of the work of these scholars that
a comprehensive dialectical theory of the female voice can
be attempted.

The female voice in Old French lyric is found in many
song types. The <u>pastourelle</u> (or male-female dialogue in a
rustic setting) has a remarkable development: more than a
hundred examples survive. Monologues in strophic <u>canso</u>
style carry laments of unmarried women who sing of the loss
or departure of a lover. The woman may blame herself, or
social events such as the crusades:

>Jherusalem, grant damage me fais
>Qui m'as tolu ce que je plus amoie,[55]

or she may be unwillingly cloistered and lament her single
life as a nun. The song of the unhappily married woman, the
<u>chanson de malmariée</u>, often takes a dance form of <u>rondo</u> or
<u>carole</u>, with a refrain. The scenario of that song includes
a hated husband, gossips, and the hoped-for or actual
lover. In other songs, satire and fantasy provide material
for the female voice. A small corpus of twenty "weaving
songs" or <u>chansons de toile</u> in archaic language and epic
lines of ten syllables, with a pause frequently after the
fourth,

>"Ma douce dame, ne le vos puis noier:
>Je ai amé un cortois soudoier,
>Le preu Henri, qui tant fet a proisier . . ."[56]

is unique to the French corpus, although the compressed
lyric drama is similar to the Spanish <u>romance</u> in its epic
tonality. While we can here only sample the wide range of
this large corpus (more than two hundred <u>trouvères</u> and over
two thousand lyrics) we can recognize the poetic conventions
of the female voice.

Dialogue in the French *pastourelle* lacks the witty verbal display and conscious irony of such Provençal and Italian examples as Marcabru's "L'autrier 'jost una sebissa," Guiraut de Riquier's series of lyrics beginning "L'autre jorn m'anava" and Cielo D'Alcamo's "Rosa fresca aulentissima." The French *pastourelle* is a song of male sexual prowess; narrative plot takes precedence over verbal texture. The shepherdess is described as a "gentil pastorele" or a "dame simple et coie . . . bele et polie / cors bien fet, gorge jolie" (R1698/ 265.1425). She often carries the signs of conventional female beauty, "Les euz verz, le chief blondel / . . . La color fresche et vermeille." She describes herself in the same affirmative manner:

> Je sui sade et brunete
> Et jone pucelete
> S'ai coleur vermeillete
> Euz verz, bele bouchete. [57]

She is young—the age of thirteen is specified in one lyric, "Treze ans a que je fui nee." The knight may offer gifts to her:

> Si vous donrai riche don
> Escarlate et peliçon
> La çainture de deus tors [58]

which she may accept or turn down. the following lyric shows a young woman hesitant to enter an affair. but willing to be conquered by a knight's "biau senblant":

> L'autrier, quant je chevauchoie
> Desouz l'onbre d'un präel,
> Trouvai gentil pastorele,
> Les euz verz, le chief blondel,
> Vestue d'un blïaudel,
> La color fresche et vermeille,
> De roses fet un chapel.
>
> Je la saluai, la bele;
> Ele me respont briement.
> "Bele, avez vous point d'ami
> Qui vous face biau senblant?"
> Tantost respont en riant:
> "Nenil voir, chevalier sire,
> Mes g'en aloie un querant."
>
> "Bele, puis qu'ami n'avez,
> Dites, se vos m'amerez."
> Ele respont conme sage:
> "Oïl, se vous m'espousez,
> Lors ferez voz volentez;
> Et se querez autre chose,
> Ce seroit desloiautez."

"Bele, ce lessiez ester,
N'avons cure d'espouser,
Ainz demerrons nostre joie
Tant com la porrons mener,
De besier et d'acoler;
Et je vous ferai fiance
Que je n'avrai autre a per."

"Sire, vostre biau senblant
Va mon cuer si destraignant,
Vostres sui, que que nus die,
Des cestui jour en avant."
N'ala pas .iii. pas en avant,
Entre mes braz l'ai sesie
Deseur l'erbe verdoiant. [59]

Not all shepherdesses were easily persuaded; and some even give the knight the slip, as in the following <u>pastourelle</u> with a surprise ending, "L'autrier tout seus chevauchoie," wherein the father of the shepherdess plays a supporting role. Rustic games, dances, and musical instruments played by groups of young men and women are features of some Old French <u>pastourelles</u>.

L'autrier tout seus chevauchoie
Toute ma sente pleniere;
Delez l'unbre d'un boschet
La trouvé gentil bergiere;
Lez li m'assis o lie chiere.
Puis li dis: "Dex vous saut, bergiere;
Pour tant com ci vous ai vëue
Vous aim plus que ne faz ma mere."

Ele ne fu pas esbahie.
Si dist: "Dex vos saut, vassal;
Entrez en vostre chemin
Et montez sus vo cheval.
Gardez que ne mi faciez mal,
Car mes peres est en l'aree,
Ou il esploite a son jornal.
Certes, se il vos vëoit ore,
Mult tost i penseroit a mal."

"Bele, n'aiez pas pöor,
Ne sonmes pas janglëor;
Pour vous que tant par ai chiere,
Voudrai devenir pastor,
Si vous donrai riche don,
Escarlate et peliçon
La çainture de deus tors:
S'irons cueillir la vïolete
Et si serons riches d'amors,
Et si serez plus joliete
Que l'alöete au point du jor."

> "Sire, bien m'avez conquise,
> Fetes de moi vo plesir;
> G'irai mes bestes acueillir,
> Et vous remandrez un pou ci."
> Cele s'en entre en un essart,
> Et cil li gete un douz regart;
> Vers son pere s'en va la bele,
> Et il demeure con musart.
> L'ame de lui soit la honie,
> Quant la bele li eschapa.[60]

The theme of an unwilling girl conquered by force is present in a number of <u>pastourelles</u>. In the song "En ma forest entrai l'autrier" the young woman is guarding her lambs as night comes on, and she is in shadow. Her clothing is described in negatives: no sleeveless jumper, furred tunic, kerchief or hat. She is alone, her clothing open, singing a song that the trouvère/knight does not recognize. To her refusal, "Lessiez moi mes aigniax garder / De vostre gieu n'ai cure," he responds with action, "Par les flans l'ai saisie."

> En ma forest entrai l'autrier
> Pour moi deduire et solacier,
>   Si truis pastore gente,
> Aigniax gardoit en un vergier
> Desouz l'onbre d'une ente.
>
> N'avoit surcot ne peliçon
> Ne guimplete ne chaperon,
>   Toute estoit desfublee;
> Blanche ot la gorge et le menton
> Plus que noif seur gelee.
>
> Seule sanz compaignon estoit,
> En sa main un baston tenoit,
>   A haute voiz s'escrie:
> Une chançonete disoit,
> Mes ne m'i savoit mie.
>
> Lez li m'assis dessouz l'arbroi,
> Puis dis: "Pastoure, entent a moi,
>   Si ne t'esmaie mie;
> Se tu vens fere riens pour moi,
> De toi ferai m'amie."
>
> "Franc chevalier, lessiez m'ester,
> Je n'ai cure de moi gaber,
>   Vez ci la nuit oscure.
> Lessiez moi mes aigniax garder,
> De vostre gien n'ai cure."

> Quant je l'öi ensi parler,
> Lez li m'asis sanz arester,
> Par les flans l'ai saisie;
> Tant la besai et acolai
> Qu'ele devint m'amie. [61]

The song of the unhappily married woman is one of the most popular of the medieval period; indeed, Rudolf Dähne claims that it is the most popular dramatic lyric theme.[62] The complaints against the husband are many: he is old and ugly. he mistreats his wife in many forms: he locks her up, beats her, neglects her, punishes her by not feeding or clothing her. He is certainly jealous of her "ami," who is often a shadowy character, more hoped-for than actual, for her description of him is less specific than that of the husband. Her hostility is often mingled with humorous malevolence; she is gleeful about "getting even":

> 'Por coi me bait mes maris.
> laisette!
>
> Je ne li ai rienz mesfait
> ne riens ne li ai mesdit
> fors c'acolleir mon amin
> soulette.
> > por coi me bait mes maris,
> > laisette!
>
> Et c'il ne mi lait dureir
> ne bone vie meneir,
> je lou ferai cous clameir,
> a certes.
> > por coi me bait mes maris,
> > laisette!
>
> Or sai bien que je ferai
> et coment m'an vangerai:
> avec mon amin geirai
> nuette.
> > por coi me bait mes maris,
> > laisette!' [63]

Her vengeance is planned and sweet. The "frame" form of the <u>pastourelle</u> may be the means for introducing the <u>malmariée</u> character:

> L'autrier par une anjornee
> chivachoie mon chamin,
> novelette mariee
> trovai leis un gal foilli,
> batue de son mari:
> si en ot lou cuer doulant
> et por ceu aloit dixant
> cest motet par auradie

>   'ne me bates mie,
> maleuroz maris.
>   vos ne m'aveis pas norrie.'⁶⁴

Often the unhappy wife threatens to take a lover as a means of asserting power in an intolerable situation. Death of the husband is frankly desired:

> Pour quoi me va chastoiant
> ne blamant
> mes maris?
> se plus me va corroucant
> ne tençant
> li chetis
> li biaus li blons li jolis
> si m'avra.
>   li jalous
>   envious
>   de cor rous
>   morra
>   et li dous
>   savourous
>   amourous
>   m'avra. ⁶⁵

The dance pattern of repetition in rhythm and rhyme gives this refrain song a popular and typically woman's voice sound.

The lament of a single woman calling for a lover uses several motifs. She may blame her loss on her own severe attitude:

> Lasse, por quoi refusai
> Celui qui tant m'a amee?
> Lonc tens a a moi musé
> Et n'i a merci trouvee.
> Lasse, si trés dur cuer ai!
>   Qu'en dirai?
>   Forsenee
> Fui, plus que desvee
> Quant le refusai.
>   G'en ferai
> Droit a son plesir.
> S'il m'en daigne oïr. ⁶⁶

or ask for divine protection and safe return for her lover gone to fight the Saracen in the Holy Land:

> Chanterai por mon corage
> Que je vueil reconforter;
> Car avec mon grant damage
> Ne vueill morir n'afoler,
> Quant de la terre sauvage

>   Ne voi mes nul retorner.
>   Ou cil est qui rasoage
>   Mes max quant g'en oi parler.
>   Dex, quant crieront outree,
>   Sire, aidiez au pelerin
>   Por qui sui espöantee.
>   Car felon sont Sarrazin.

This French "crusade lament" has the motif of clothing given as a token of love in absence:

>   Sa chemise qu'ot vestue
>   M'envoia pour enbracier.
>   La nuit, quant s'amor m'argue,
>   La met delés moi couchier
>   Mult estroit a ma char nue
>   Pour mes maux assöagier.[67]

Another form of lament for a lover is the "nun's lament" in which a young woman sings about her unwilling confinement in a convent. This song may also have the "frame" voice of a narrator in the <u>pastourelle</u> style; a male voice introduces the singing or lamenting woman:

>   Quant ce vient en mai ke rose est panie,
>   je l'alai coillir per grant druërie.
>   En pou d'oure oï une voix serie
>   lonc un vert bouset, pres d'une abïete.
>   Je sant les douls mals leis ma centurete
>   Malois soit de Deu ki me fist nonnete!

After the introduction of her voice in the first refrain, she is the speaker for three stanzas:

>   Ki nonne me fist, Jesus lou maldie!
>   Je di trop envis vespres ne complies:
>   car asseiz aing miels bonne compaingnie,
>   ke est deduissans et amerousete,

and to close the lyric the narrator/poet again speaks, telling us the happy conclusion:

>   Quant ses amis ot la parolle oïe
>   de joie tressaut, le cuers li fremie,
>   a la porte en vient de celle abaïe,
>   si en jetait fors sa douce amïete.[68]

In another "nun's lament" the monk/lover is addressed in the terms of affection usually given to the "ami":

>   ceste chansonette
>   dixoit la nonette
>   "longue demoree
>   faites, frans moinnes loialz.

>   se plus suis nonette,
>   ains ke soit li vespres,
>   je morai des jolis malz."[69]

A group of twenty dramatic lyrics in epic language and style tell the stories of young women and married women in love with knights occupied more with war and tournaments than with thoughts of love. Their common epithet is "bele": Bele Amelot, Bele Aiglentine, Bele Doette, Bele Emmelot, Bele Yolanz, Bele Ysabiaux, and they are pictured sitting in a room or castle tower with their mothers, sewing or weaving cloth. Their stories have much variety, and we will here mention several briefly to show the range of plot situation and outcome:

1. Bele Aiglentine, unable to do her sewing, confesses to her mother that she is pregnant by Count Henry. The mother asks about the possibility of marriage, and advises the daughter to go to Henry to ask him to marry her. This done, the daughter is carried off "en son pais" to live as a rich countess. This sweet story will be given in full, as an example of the style of the <u>chanson de toile</u>, its refrains, assonance, decasyllabic line, and frank, evocative treatment of its theme. The refrain "Or orrez ja / Comment la bele Aiglentine esploita." follows each stanza.

>   Bele Aiglentine en roial chamberine
>   Devant sa dame cousoit une chemise:
>   Ainc n'en sot mot quant bone amor l'atise.
>   Or orrez ja
>   Comment la bele Aiglentine esploita.
>
>   Devant sa dame cousoit et si tailloit;
>   Mes ne coust mie si com coudre soloit:
>   El s'entroublie, si se point en son doit.
>   La soe mere mout tost s'en aperçoit.
>
>   "Bele Aiglentine, deffublez vo sorcot,
>   Je voil veoir desoz vostre gent cors."
>   "Non ferai, dame, la froidure est la morz."
>
>   "Bele Aiglentine, q'avez a empirier
>   Que si vos voi palir et engroissier?"
>   "Ma douce dame, ne le vos puis noier:
>
>   "Je ai amé un cortois soudoier,
>   Le preu Henri, qui tant fet a proisier.
>   S'onques m'amastes, aiez de moi pitié."
>
>   "Bele Aiglentine, vos prendra il Henris?"
>   "Ne sai voir, dame, car onques ne li quis."
>   "Bele Aiglentine, or vos tornez de ci.

> "Tot ce li dites que ge li mant Henri,
> S'il vos prendra ou vos lera einsi."
> "Volontiers, dame", la bele respondi.
>
> Bele Aiglentine s'est tornee de ci
> Et est venue droit a l'ostel Henri.
> Li quens Henris se gisoit en son lit.
> Or orrez ja que la bele li dit
>
> "Sire Henri, velliez vos ou dormez?
> Ja vos requiert Aiglentine au vis cler,
> Se la prendrez a moullier et a per."
> "Oïl" dit Henris, "onc joie n'oi mes tel."
>
> Oit le Henris, molt joianz en devint:
> Il fet monter chevaliers trusqu'a vint;
> Si enporta la bele en son païs
> Et l'espousa, riche contesse en fist.[70]

The final refrain is changed in theme to make a coda to the song, "Grant joie a / Li quens Henris quant bele Aiglentine a." But not all the "beles" have as happy a resolution to their story as does Aiglentine.

   2. Bele Doette, reading at her window, sees a squire bringing news of her absent lord. The news is of death at a tournament. She vows to become a nun at Saint Pol and to build an abbey for other lovers. The refrain is one line, "E or en ai dol."[71]

   3. Bele Yolanz is in her room sewing a fine robe for her lover. He hears her refrain song, "Dex, tant est douz li nons d'amors: / ja n'en cuidai sentir dolors," and comes into her room. They agree to dismiss the gossips from their thoughts and find happiness in love.

   4. Bele Ydoine, faithful to her love for Garsilion, suffers beatings and imprisonment ordered by her father the king to cure her rebellion against his wishes. After three years in the keep, she is rescued by her lover.

   5. Bele Argentine, wife of Count Guis, gives him six sons. He falls in love with young Sabine, and sends his wife away. Her sons are "remplis de vaillance, de sens de l'honneur et de générosité." They are hired by the German emperor in whose land Argentine has found refuge, and they take their mother back home and reinstate her with her husband. The refrain compresses the plot, "Qui est unie à un méchant mari, / souvent s'en sépare le coeur trists."

   6. Bele Beatris, engaged to marry Duke Henry, is pregnant by her lover Hugo. She sends a message to Hugo, who takes her away to his castle. The angry Duke Henry confronts the father and mother, who counsel calm. The Duke

returns to his castle where he dies of love. Again the refrain encapsulates the story, "Bien sont asavore li mal / c'on trait por fine amor loial."

The *chansons de toile* treat the love theme from the woman's standpoint. She may be married or unmarried, but we see her experience through her own desires. Often her will is strong and she triumphs over obstacles of mistreatment, absence, and death. Representative of a precourtly love ethic, the *chansons de toile* were woven into the narratives of courtly romances such as *Guilaume de Dole*, *Le Roman de la Violette*, and *Fauvel*, where they lend a flavor of archaism in manners and language.

A single manuscript from the early fourteenth century contains nineteen French lyrics, all anonymous, in a Lorraine dialect in the musical rhythm called *estampie* (Occitan: *estampida*). The common theme of these satirical songs is hopeless love. We have six songs of this form in Occitan, the most famous being the "Kalenda Maya" of Raimbaut de Vaqueiras. Of the French *estampies*, only one uses the female voice, the comic "C'an feme ce fie." In five *coblas doblas* (two cinquains with matching rhymes) the poet/lover gives general advice on love, then he tells his personal experience with his unfaithful *amie*. The issue is money. When he approaches her with empty pockets, she rejects him and indicts him for villainy:

>   Kant veux voir m'amie.
>   Et n'ai point d'argent,
>   Molt iriement
>   Me dit: Vai t'an
>   Je ne te conois mie!
>
>   Ains ne t'amai
>   Ne ne ferai,
>   De voir lou sai.
>   Fu de ci, ou je te ferrai!
>   Si grant despit ai
>   Et averai,
>   Kan me quiers vilonie! [72]

The female speaker is characterized as a mercenary shrew, a comic figure whose violence contrasts with the mild and rational tone of the male speaker. He pronounces abstractions and calls on the Virgin Mary for help, favorably comparing the deity to the worthless human female.

The *reverdie* is a minor genre of eight to ten extant lyrics whose theme is love in the springtime, with a *descriptio puellae*, a detailed head-to-toe portrait of personal features and clothing. Flowers, birds, and early morning in the garden are motifs of this song. Among the most charming examples is the anonymous "Volez vos que je vos chant," because the details of dress and figure become a surrealistic picture like a hand-painted miniature. The lady is riding on a golden saddle which has three rose trees to shade her. She meets a knight who asks her parentage and she gives the fanciful response:

> "de France sui la loee
> du plus haut parage.
>
> Li rosignox est mon pere,
> qui chante sor la ramee
> el plus haut boscage.
> la seraine ele est ma mere,
> qui chante en la mer salee
> el plus haut rivage."[73]

The woman of the <u>reverdie</u> is doll-like, and diminutives are used in the description of her, as in this lyric of Colin Muset:

> Sospris sui d'une amorette
> D'une jone pucelette:
> Bele est et blonde et blanchette
> Plus que n'est une erminette . . . [74]

A folkloric motif in the female voice in Old French is that of three women speaking in one lyric. Whereas a dialogue works well for presenting two opposing views, three voices can present a progression of attitudes. In a discussion of marriage or the treatment of lovers, various alternatives can be shown to which the audience can react with favor or disfavor. On the perennial question of lover versus husband, the following song's three female speakers express three possibilities. The song is in the "frame" style with its male voice introduction: a poet/narrator encounters three newly married women talking in a rural setting:

> Pancis amerouzement
> de Tornai parti l'autrierr;
> en un pre lons un destour
> vi trois dames ombroier.
> mariees de novel:
> chascune or un vert chapel.
> la moinnee a dit ansi
>   "je servirai mon mari
>   lealment en leu d'ami."
>
> Li ainnee an ot irour,
> se li dit sans atargier
> "damedex vos dont mal jour,
> nos volez vos asaier?
> au cuer ne m'est mie bel."
> dou poing an son haterel

>   l'ala maintenant ferir.
>   "je ferai novel ami
>   an despit de mon mari."
>
>   La moienne par baudour
>   fu vestue au tens d'este
>   d'un riche drap de colour,
>   d'un vert qui fait a louer.
>   en avoit robe et mantel
>   et chantoit cest chant novel,
>   si ke je l'ai bien oi:
>   "s'on trovast leal ami,
>   ja n'eusse pris mari."[75]

The youngest represents marital loyalty; the oldest, violently angry at this opinion, reports that she is ready to take a lover; while the middle one caps the argument with a witty rejoinder that, if there were faithful lovers, one would not ever have to marry. Opinion one supports the husband, opinion two supports the lover, but the third opinion casts suspicion on both previous opinions.

The multiple personae of the female speaker in Old French lyric include, as we have seen in this brief review, 1) a blonde, grey-eyed shepherdess overheard singing a snatch of song in a country setting, 2) a young nun cursing her fate or calling for a monk/lover, 3) a young woman praying for the safe return of her lover from the Crusade, or blaming the Church for his absence, 4) a married woman, defaming her husband:

>   He Dieu je n'ai pas mari
>   Du tot a mon gre
>   Il n'a cortoisie en li
>   Ne jolivete.[76]

gleefully announcing or planning her unfaithfulness with a lover, 5) a mercenary and violent shrew, 6) a fairy-like creature dressed in flowers sitting on a golden saddle with three rose trees for a sunshade, and 7) an old-fashioned lady sitting in a castle room, absorbed in her love for a soldier, a man of few words and no courtly lover.

The female persona in Italian lyric is found in a corpus of about fifty dramatic lyrics, and is similar to French and Provençal lyric style with some special qualities of its own. The Italian corpus is particularly interesting because the impulse toward future European lyric can be seen here. A mere thirteen of the songs of this group are monologues. They are vehicles for the voice of complaint and lament. Only one of the monologues is humorous, whereas the much more numerous dialogues and tenzoni are characterized by humor, either light and teasing, or open, rude invective. We find the conventional lament of the abandoned woman on the beach watching ships sail away with her lover to war or commerce. One lyric shows the motif of jealousy toward another woman, a motif extremely rare in medieval lyric, almost non-existent. Since the group of monologues in Italian is small, I will mention each of them in a brief review.

Two sonnets are ascribed to La Compiuta Donzella, the only 'named' woman poet surviving in early Italian lyric. Medieval manuscripts mention a 'Nina siciliana' and attribute a <u>tenzone</u> to her, but modern scholars do not follow this attribution. The speakers of both sonnets by La Compiuta Donzella firmly repudiate the prospect of marriage. In her lyric "A la stagion che 'l mondo foglia e fiora," a nature introduction precedes a short statement about the unhappiness of the woman, caused by her father's plan to marry her against her will:

> Ca lo mio padre m'ha messa 'n errore,
> e tenemi sovente in forte doglia:
> donar mi vole a mia forza segnore,
>
> ed io di ciò non ho disio né voglia,
> e 'n gran tormento vivo a tutte l'ore;
> però non mi ralegra fior né foglia.[77]

The contrast of joy in nature and the social world around her with her own unhappy state reminds us of the Latin poem from the Cambridge collection, "Levis exsurgit zephirus," a woman's song in the same contemplative manner. Both poems have the flavor of learned rhetorical devices, as we see from the closing lines of the Latin poem:

> Tu saltim, veris gratia,
> Exaudi et considera
> Frondes, flores et gramina,
> Nam mea languet anima.[78]

In the Latin, a double verb and triple object slow the movement and fix the attention on the contrastive element, to which the "a" sounds of the final line add equal force to her sorrow. In the Italian, the iconographic "fior ne foglia" closes the poem with the words of the first line, in the same position, framing her sorrow with the contrastive element. The unwilling bride of Compiuta Donzela's sonnet "Lasciar voria lo mondo e Dio servire" condemns the vanity of the world and the custom of marriage. She prefers the service of Christ to the unknown master her father may choose. Her anxiety on the prospect of marriage is expressed in the final line, "non saccio a cui mi vol dar per isposa."[79]

The Sicilian poet Rainaldo D'Aquino wrote two laments in the direct speech of the grieving woman. "Gia mai non mi conforto" is a crusade lament which reveals its dependence on Marcabru's "A la fontana del vergier," only here the king is "Lo 'mperadore" (Frederick II in 1228) and not the <u>reys Lozoicx</u> (Louis VII of France in 1147). The sequence of blame is less detailed in the Sicilian lyric, and the Cross is added to the list:

> La croce salva la gente
> e me face disviare,
> la croce mi fa dolente
> e non mi val Kio pregare.
> Oi croce pellegrina,
> perchè m'ài si distrutta?

and later she refers to the lover, in an echo of the Provençal lyric,

> Quando la croce pigliao.
> certo no lo mi pensai
> quelli che tanto m'amao. 80

The convention of ships in the port and a message to the poet requesting that he take the song to Soria give local settings to the common theme. In the much more effective Provençal lyric, the poet removes himself after his introduction of the woman speaker.

In Rainaldo D'Aquino's "Ormai quando flore," we see a young woman deliberating with herself about whether to give in to her lover's advances. She is of two minds, and the pain is great. She prays she may <u>not</u> give in, because she wants a quiet love without scandal. This poem has an echo of the refrain of another Latin poem, the "Pervigilium Veneris," a late Latin anonymous lyric that has both classical and non-classical elements.[81] The long nature introduction of the Italian lyric links the two poems. The Italian poet continues:

> Vedendo quell'ombrina - del fresco bosco,
> ben cognosco - ca cortamente
> serà gaudente - l'amor che mi china.
>
> /Mi/ china, ch'eo so amata
> e già mai non amai:
> ma 'l tempo mi 'namura.[82]

The passage echoes in theme and form the insistent "Cras amet qui nunquam amavit quique amavit cras amet" of the Latin lyric. The position of the passage in the Italian-- the center of the lyric--gives it major importance, and the story is peripheral to Nature's love song. In the contest of Nature and Society for the girl's mind, Nature is about to take the lead.

The anonymous lyric "Oi lassa 'Namorata" is a rather standard type of the abandoned woman suffering the pangs of rage and desire. This poem has a message for the rival, which adds a note of humor:

> Va canzonetta fina,
> al buono aventuroso,
> ferilo a la corina
> se 'l truovi disdegnoso;
> no 'l ferir di rapina,
> che sia troppo gravoso;
> ma ferila chi 'l tene,
> aucidela sen fallo!
> Poi sacc/i/o c'a me vene
> lo viso del cristallo
> e saro fuor di pene
> e avrò alegreza e gallo.

The almost total absence of the theme of women fighting each other for a lover's attention or expressing their jealousy of a rival is remarkable when we consider the youth of the adolescent girls before marriage and the prevalence of poems of married women and their lovers. The figure of the "girlfriend" is generally positive in poems both by men and women poets of the medieval period.

The first stanza of this poem "Oi lassa 'namorata" has an image that is worth noting, since other examples come to mind. The girl feels her loss as a blow to her pride, and her pride is "splitting her heart," "ed or mi mena orgoglio / lo cor me fende e taglia." The image of fragmentation as extremely painful and yet a frequent experience occurs in both the prose and poetry of women in many areas. A statement of the poetics of this poem is also found in the first stanza. She will speak "as love bids me," that is, from the heart, without intellectual interference. She thus creates the illusion that her speech is artless and natural, as though she could arrange twelve lines in a strict rhyme scheme "artlessly." I think the stanza is worth quoting:

> Oi lassa 'namorata,
> contar vo' la mia vita
> e dire ogne fiata
> come l'amor mi 'nvita,
> ch'io son, sanza peccata,
> d'assai pene guernita
> per uno c'amo e voglio
> e non l'agio in mia baglia
> si com'avere soglio

> però pato travaglia
> ed or mi mena orgoglio,
> lo cor me fende e taglia.

"Artless" female speech can provide a technique whereby dispassionate observation of a human heart can co-exist with the expression of deep feeling. In this stanza she can look into both her mind and her heart, and report her experience of injustice and pride without divorcing them from her feelings, i.e. making them into abstractions.

Two anonymous laments on the subject of death follow, and their titles show that they are exercises in conventional poetic rhetoric. "Dispietata morte e fera" and "Morte fera e dispietata."[84] They are well within the conventions of the address and complaint to death. Four other courtly monologues may be included in this group of "art songs" in a female voice. Three of these are addressed to "meo sire" and to "dolce meo sire." They express in the conventions of fin' amors the unhappiness of the lady who has done nothing wrong and is still full of compliments for the object of her sweet hopes.

There remain two monologues in the persona of married women. One is a malmaritata which plainly tells the woman's side of the home warfare; if he is not going to give her the solace she needs, it will be his fault if she seeks it with another man. It has the delightful word "scornaclabele," a very early attestation of the modern "scorniciare," "to remove from a frame." The poem, "Apicè sia 'l mal mari" is found in the Memoriali Bolognesi, along with many anonymous women's voice poems. The poems were written in the margins of official manuscripts.[85]

The last poem of this section is a humorous sonnet by Rustico Filippi, "Oi dolce mio marito Aldobrandino," in which the wife soothes her husband's ruffled feelings about the neighbor's doublet accidently found in his bed. She ends her coaxing with the ancient joke that the neighbor "did nothing to her that she did not like."[86]

If the monologue is the vehicle for lament, the dialogue is the vehicle for discussion and comedy. The closer a poem's structure of direct speech reaches either pole the more visible is the rule. For instance, in a poem of shared speech, if a narrator introduces a lady who then occupies the whole poem, her speech will be a lament. But if, at the other extreme, a single line has two or even three changes of voice, we have the "lazzo" effect of comic patter, rapid and funny. In the center of these two extremes are the measured poems that discuss issues of love in abstract terms, or that treat questions of dispute between two people, either about marriage or about leaving. When the balanced dispute becomes comic, language reflects the imbalance in social position of the two partners to the debate. The alternation will be from idealized, inflated terms of fin' amor in the male voice, to realistic, deflated responses from the female. There are notable examples of all these types in the very rich Italian lyric, and I will be able to mention only a few of them, concluding this section with some comments on the lyrics of Dante.

An anonymous lyric from the Sicilian school, "Di dolor convien cantare" shows the malmaritata lament framed by an introduction and a conclusion spoken by her grieving lover.[87] She describes her misery and the severe beatings her husband gives her. Curiously, she speaks like the "last Duchess" of Robert Browning's dramatic monologue, "My Last Duchess," in reverse, that is, she says that if anything makes her joyful she must hide it from her husband, because it is precisely her joy that makes him angry, and someone must intervene so that he will stop tormenting her. In another poem on the malmaritata theme, "Per lo marito c'o rio," also shared with the voice of her lover, the woman blames her husband for neglecting her so that she seeks love elsewhere, and she repeats this message openly to her lover, saying that he has her only because of her husband's anger.[88] She asks for advice about the neighbor vecchia who disturbs her, and she assures her lover that her complaints do not mean she has another man in mind; she is faithful to him.

A series of poems that are less dramatic and more conversational, in which speech is shared equally within the poem between male and female voice, show a balance of reason and emotion in the treatment of standard themes. In Giacomino Pugliese's "Donna, di voi mi lamento," a husband talks over his suspicions about her fidelity with his wife.[89] In "L'altr'ieri fui in parlamento," an unmarried woman begs her lover to take her away so she will not have to marry the man her father has chosen.[90] The lover counsels her to marry her father's chosen groom, but to count on his love and loyalty to console her. In Mazzeo di Ricco da Messina's 'Lo core innamorato,'' a woman asks for assurance of fidelity from her lover.[91] Likewise, honor and fidelity are the subject of a dialogue between a lady and her lover in "L'amor fa una donna amare" of the Sicilian poet Compagnetto da Prato.[92] The theme of the partida with its pains and its promises forms the subject of three songs: "L'anghososa partença" from the Memoriali Bolognesi (government documents with poems inserted in the margins). the anonymous Sicilian "Non m'aven d'allegranza," and "Dolze meo drudo eh vatène" of King Frederick II.[93] In these examples, the woman's voice is either the first part of a two-part division or an unequal number of stanzas (two out of five). All of them balance the pain of parting with assurances of faithful love. All are canzoni.

The most measured and balanced of all the forms in Italian is the stately sonnet series in which the man's or the woman's voice occupies an entire sonnet. The language is polite, although not exclusively of fin'amor; a six-sonnet series by Guittone D'Arezzo beginning "Villana donna, non mi ti disdire" has a "villana donna" and a "villan parldore" hurling invective at each other; but the space between speeches allows each speech to have weight and dignity in spite of diction.[94] This series is a parody of courtly love and is delightful. The other tenzone of the corpus, by Amico di Dante, La Compiura Donzella, and anonymous (but attributed in medieval manuscripts to a Nina Siciliana) are discussions of faith, love, and gentle speech. The tenzone of La Compiuta Donzella is particularly interesting because its first sonnet inspired another by Mastro Torregiano di Firenze, "Esser donzella di trovare dotta."[95]

Three songs show a young woman pleading for a husband during a conversation with her parents. All three are anonymous, two are from the Memoriale Bolognesi. One of the latter poems is remarkable for its father-daughter dialogue; a rare example only seen in the Italian corpus. The pastora of some French pastourelles calls a nearby father or brothers to chase away the knight, but these minor characters usually have no lines of direct speech. The poem "Babbo meo dolce, con' tu mal fai" gives the father the third of four stanzas.[96] He advises his daughter not to make too much of the fact that he is keeping her at home in the family, but to pray to God and he may get her a husband. A longer and more detailed conversation between a daughter who wants to marry and a mother who thinks she is still too young is in the lyric 'Mamma, lo temp' è venuto." The mother warns of possible death (probably meaning death in childbirth) "tosto podriss' esser morta / s'usassi con hom, ben lo sai."[97] The girl mentions the hero Roland and "lo bon duxo Morando," and her own timid but strong desires. The third song of this motif "request for a husband" is the anonymous Sicilian "Part'io mi cavalcava." In an abbreviated introduction the narrator overhears a young woman and her mother talking in a dialogue that moves from polite tones to invective.[98] The mother says to her daughter:

> "Oi figlia, non pensai
> si fosse mala tosa, . . .

and the daughter:

> "Oi vecchia trenta cuoia,
> non mi stare in tenzone . . .

Five comic songs are at the farthest extreme from the monologue-lament. They alternate male and female voices more closely and for a larger portion of the lyric than any other songs. One, "Becchin' amor! Che vuo', falso tradito?" by Cecco Angiolieri, alternates male and female speech within each line of the fourteen line sonnet.[99] The other songs alternate voices in each stanza, but the stanzas are generally short, and there are enough of them to set up a strong sparring rhythm of attack and defense. Comedy is carried through in themes and diction; dialectal speech is a typical feature. The <u>contrasto</u> "Rosa fresca aulentissima" from the Sicilian school (attributed to Cielo D'Alcamo by Contini, but listed as anonymous in Panvini) alternates courtly and outlandish speech, recalling Raimbaut de Vaqueiras' "Domna, tant vos ai pregada."[100] Several types of <u>repetitio</u> are used in this poem, from the chaining of verse to verse by last and first line links, a catalogue, and a fugue familiar in today's children's rhymes and stories: she will escape by going to a nunnery, but he will become a monk,

> Se tanto addivenissemi, tagliàrami le treze,
>   e comsore m'arenno a una magione,
>   avanti che m'artocchi 'n la persone.
>
> Se tu comsore arenneti, donna col viso cleri,
>   a lo mostero vènoci e rènnomi confreri.

She tells him to search the earth and find another lady,

> Cerca la terra ch'este gran/n/e assai,
> chiù bella donna di me troverai.

and he replies with his catalogue:

> "Cercat'ajo Calabr[i]a, Toscana e Lombardia,
> Puglia, Constantinopoli, Genoa, Pisa e Soria,
> Lamagna e Babilonïa /e/ tut/t/a Barberia:

but he cannot find her equal. He gives his poetics of conquest:

> "Di ciò che dici, vitama, neiente non ti bale,
> ca de le tuo parabole fatto n'ho ponti e scale.
> Penne penzasti met/t/ere, sonti cadute l'ale;
>   e dato t'ajo la bolta sot/t/ana.
>   Dunque, se po/t/i, tèniti villana."

He has "made a ladder and a bridge of her words," but she cares little,

> Prezo le tue parabole meno che d'un zitiello,

his words are "less than a boy's" to her. Finally, the exhausted suitor swears on a Bible (that he happened to have with him) to marry his love, and his final, blunt request,

"Arcompli mi' talento in caritate / che l'arma me ne sta in suttilitate" wins an apology and a good natured reconciliation in the bed, in a comic *carpe diem*, "A lo letto ne gimo a la bon'ura / chè chissà cosa n'è data in ventura." It is no wonder that this verbal duel became widely popular.

Five lyrics illustrate the form in which female speech plays a small but important part. In all five the direct female speech occurs in the center of the lyric, in the second part of the second or third stanza. Three of the five songs are *partidas*, two written by Giacomino Pugliese and one anonymous. In the lyric "La dolze cera piagente" the woman scolds her lover about leaving her:

> Messer, se venite a gire,
> non facciate adimoranza
> che non e bona usanza
> lasciar l'amore e partire. [101]

This *partida* has a happy ending. Evidently her admonition took effect, because he did not go far, and came back full of love and happy to see her again among her women friends, "lo cor mi trae di martire / e ralegrami la mente." The second lyric, "Isplendiente stella d'albore," is much longer than the first, with eight stanzas. The male speaks in the early part of the poem, and the lady only at the close of the sixth strophe. She forswears games and dancing, and will become a recluse when he is gone:

> "Se vai, mio sire, e fai dimoranza,
> ve' ch' io m'arendo e faccio altra vita,
> già mai non entro in gioco né in danza
> ma sto rinchiusa piú che romita."

The anonymous Sicilian lyric "Membrando l'amoroso dipartiri" has many of the conventions of the *partida*; the commendation to God, sighing and fainting, and in this tone the lover/narrator who is leaving, quotes the lady:

> "se vai, amore, me lasci in tormento;
> io n'averò pensiero e cordoglienza
> e disio so/lo/ di venire a tivi;
> si come audivi - che vai lonrana parte,
> da me si parte - la gioia del meo core;
> se vai, amore, - lo meo cor lasci in parte".

Ardent promises and claims on the lover's part close this conventional *partida*.

The last two poems of this group, "Un nobil e gentil imaginare" of Paolo Lanfranchi, and "In un boschetto trova' pasturella" of Guido Cavalcanti, are dream visions. They are sweetly musical; each line contains key words of *fin' amor* such as garden, heart, nightingale, kiss, and the *pastorela* of Cavalcante adds angels singing. In each lyric, the words of the female speaker are encouraging to the male. Her soft tones are echoed later in the poem, transmuted to a bird (in the first) and to an angel (in the second). I will give both the woman's speech and the transformed speech, since this dolce note signals a change in lyric style. Lanfranchi's poem begins with the dream vision. The poet is in a garden (in his sleep) and dreams that his lady is there. They kiss and embrace and she says:

> . . . Tu m'hai in tu bailia
> fa' di me, o amor, cio che ti pare

then a nightingale sings:

> Securamente per vostro amor canto.[104]

In the Cavalcanti *pastorela*, the shepherdess says, in response to the request for love:

> "Sacci, quando l'augel pia
> allor disia -- 'l me' cor drudo avere"

and the angel sang:

> Or è stagione
> di questa pasturella gio' pigliare.[105]

and the poem closes with the poet so entranced "che 'l die d'amore--mi parea vedere." The range of women's voice speech has come to a new development with dolce stil novo and its transformation into a soft and sweet tone figured by birds and angels.

Notes to Chapter 3

1   The numbers in this section refer to lyrics in Sola Solé, Corpus de poesía mozárabe, employing Arabic rather than his Roman numerals.

2   Elvira Gangutia Elícegui, "Poesía griega 'de amigo' y poesía arábigo-española," Emérita 40 (1972), 329-96.

3   See especially Margit Frenk Alatorre, Las jarchas mozárabes y los comienzos de la lírica románica (Mexico City: El Colegio de México, 1975) pp. 156-8, "En la Romania pre-trovadoresca existió una vigorosa tradición lírica de tipo popular ajena a los canones clásicos, y esa lírica era predominantemente femenina: monólogo de mujer enamorada."

4   Kathleen Ashley, "The Role of the Courts and the 13th Century Portuguese Lyric," ACTA 3 (1976), 65-78.

5   The numbers of Galician-Portuguese cantigas de amigo refer to the lyrics in José Joaquim Nunes, Cantigas d'amigo dos trovadores galego-portugueses, vol. 1, employing Arabic rather than his Roman numerals.

6   Alan Deyermond, "Pero Meogo's Stags and Fountains: Symbol and Anecdote in the Traditional Lyric," Romance Philology 33 (1979), 265-283.

7   Cynthia P. Bagley, "Cantigas de Amigo and Cantigas de Amor," Bulletin of Hispanic Studies 43 (1966) 241-252.

8   The songs with lines of direct speech in a female persona in Provençal lyric may be found in standard anthologies, principally Hill and Bergin, Anthology of the Provençal Troubadours, 2nd ed., which contains about half of the poems chosen for this section. A few poems come from the anthologies of Bartsch, Nelli and Lavaud, and Anglade, and some important texts were found in Willard Trask, Medieval Lyrics of Europe. I have also used Jules Véran, Les Poétesses Provençales du moyen âge et de nos jours, and Meg Bogin, The Women Troubadours. A more thorough search in the editions of all Provençal poets would no doubt bring to light additonal songs with female speech.

9   For the meanings, physical and spiritual, of joi and jovens. see A. J. Denomy, "Jois Among the Early Troubadours: Its Meaning and Possible Source," Mediaeval Studies 13 (1951), 177-217.; also his "Jovens: the Notion of Youth Among the Troubadours, Its Meaning and Source," Mediaeval Studies 11 (1949), 1-22.

10   Gabrielle Kussler-Ratyé, "Les Chansons de la Comtesse Beatrix de Dia," Archivum Romanicum 1 (1917), 161-182, esp. p. 174.

11   Kussler-Ratyé, p. 161.

12   Véran, p. 76.

13   Karl Bartsch, Chrestomathie provençale, p. 226.

14   Kussler-Ratyé, p. 174.

15   Jean Audiau, Nouvelle anthologie des troubadours, p. 287.

16   René Nelli and René Lavaud, Les Troubadours, p. 152.

17   Hill and Bergin, Anthology, vol. 1, p. 32.

18   Kussler-Ratyé, p. 169.

19   Véran, p. 128.

20   Véran, p. 85.

21   Véran, p. 102.

22   Véran, 107.

23   Véran, p. 109.

24   Kussler-Ratyé, p. 169.

25   Nelli and Lavaud, p. 134.

26   Hill and Bergin, vol. 1, p. 70.

27   Hill and Bergin, vol. 1, p. 50.

28   Joan Ferrante, Woman as Image in Medieval Literature, (New York: Columbia Univ. Press, 1975), ii.

29   John Moore, Love in Twelfth-Century France (Philadelphia: Univ. of Pennsylvania Press, 1972). p. 87. The phrase "spectrum of attitudes" is from M. J. Valency, In Praise of Love, (New York: Macmillan, 1958) p. 143.

30   See Ibn Zaidūn's celebrated "Nuniyya" ode, with its monorhyme on the pronoun "nun," the Arabic first person plural in James Monroe, Hispano-Arabic Poetry: A Student Anthology, p. 178. Compare to this "Ab la dolchor del temps novel" of William IX, with its lines "la nostr'amor" in the third stanza, and "Nos n'avem la pessa e.l coutel," in the last. Also, a significant number of Galician-Portuguese cantigas d'amigo express a "mutual love" ethos.

31   Kussler-Ratyé, p. 134.

32   Véran, p. 117.

33   Véran, p. 158.

34   Anna Granville Hatcher, "Marcabru's 'A la fontana del vergier"' in Modern Language Notes 79 (1964) 284-95.

35   Hill and Bergin, p. 18.

36   Bartsch, Chrest. Prov., p. 226.

37   Nunes, p. 441.

38   Hill and Bergin, p. 164.

39   Hill and Bergin, p. 258.

40   Bartsch, Chrest. Prov., col. 269.

41   Carl Appel, Provenzalische Chrestomathie, p. 85.

42   I will mention only two examples: Leo Spitzer sees a primitive world of women dancing and chanting the songs men have created for them, so that the men could achieve a vicarious pleasure, ". . . Thus woman has in primitive world literature a role imposed upon her by man, answering him with the very words of longing he has suggested to her," Comparative Literature 4 (1952) 22. Frederick Golden defines the malmariée theme as "a song sung by a woman who takes her pleasures, but not her marriage, seriously, and wherever she can find them," Lyrics of the Troubadours and Trouvères (New York: Doubleday, 1973) p. 407.

43   Willard Trask, Medieval Lyrics of Europe, p. 17. Peter Dronke, The Medieval Lyric, Chapter Three, "Cantigas de Amigo."

44   Alfred Jeanroy, Histoire sommaire de la poésie occitane, (Paris: Didier, 1945), p. 78.

45   Carroll Smith-Rosenberg, "The Female World of Love and Ritual: Relations Between Women in 19th-Century America," in Signs: Journal of Women in Culture and Society, (Chicago: Univ. of Chicago Press, 1, (1975) 1-29.

46   Sophie Drinker, Music and Women (New York: Coward-McCann, 1948).

47   Véran, p. 112.

[48] The literature on the *pastourelle* includes: John Danielson (1959). Michel Zink (1972), W.T.H. Jackson (1952), W. P. Jones (1931), W. D. Paden, and E. Faral (1923). The philosophical basis of the eclogue, of which the *pastourelle* is a sub-genre, may be studied in Thomas G. Rosenmeyer, *The Green Cabinet: Theocritus and the European Pastoral Lyric*, (Berkeley: Univ. of California Press, 1969).

[49] R.J.E. Tiddy, "Satura and Satire," *English Literature and the Classics*, ed. G. S. Gordon (Oxford: Clarendon, 1912) pp. 195-227.

[50] Tiddy, p. 209.

[51] Hill and Bergin, p. 3.

[52] Hill and Bergin, p. 24.

[53] Bec, *La lyrique française au moyen âge*, vol. 2, p. 16.

[54] See the section "La Question des Origines," entry nos. 117-144 in Robert Taylor, *La Littérature occitane du moyen âge: bibliographie sélective et critique* (Toronto: Univ. of Toronto Press, 1977). The present study, based on contextuality, by-passes this question.

[55] Bec, *La Lyrique*, vol. 2, p. 10 (R191: 265.939).

[56] Bec, *La Lyrique*, vol. 2, p. 30-32.

[57] Spanke, EAL, p. 14.

[58] Spanke, EAL, p. 48.

[59] Spanke, EAL, p. 174 (R1708: 265.1037).

[60] Spanke, EAL, p. 164. (R1709: 265.1038)

[61] Spanke, EAL, p. 239 (R1257: 265.627).

[62] Rudolf Dähne, *Die Lieder der Maumariée*, Chapter One.

[63] Bec, *La Lyrique*, vol. 2, p. 166 (R1564: 265.1346).

[64] R493: 265.1031

[65] Bartsch, *Rom. und Past.*, pp. 53-54.

[66] Bec, *La Lyrique*, vol. 2, pp. 7-8 (R100: 265.990).

[67] Bec, *La Lyrique*, vol. 2, pp. 92-4 (R21: 106.4).

[68] Bec, *La Lyrique*, vol. 2, p. 20 (R1156: 265.1482).

69   Bec, La Lyrique, vol. 2, p. 55.

70   Bec, La Lyrique, vol. 2, p. 30-32.

71   Zink, Belle, pp. 77-167, all the chansons de toile, with trans. into modern French.

72   Walter O. Streng-Renkonen, Les Estampies française, (CFMA 85), pp. 26-28.

73   Bec, La Lyrique, vol. 2, p. 60.

74   Bec, La Lyrique, vol. 2, p. 63.

75   Bartsch, Rom. und Past., no. 21.

76   Bec, La Lyrique, vol. 2, p. 14.

77   Contini, vol. 2, p. 434.

78   Helen Waddell, Medieval Latin Lyrics, (Baltimore: Penguin, 1968), p. 168.

79   Contini, vol. 2, p. 435.

80   Panvini, Le Rime della scuola siciliana, no. 5.

81   Raby, Secular Latin Poetry, vol. 1.

82   Panvini, Le Rime, p. 115.

83   Panvini, Le Rime, p. 461.

84   Panvini, Le Rime, p. 492.

85   Contini, vol. 1, p. 783.

86   Contini, vol. 1, p. 783.

87   Panvini, Le Rime, p. 463.

88   Panvini, Le Rime, p. 229.

89   Carducci, Antica Lirica Italiana, p. 13.

90   Panvini, Le Rime, p. 496.

91   Panvini, Le Rime, p. 205.

92   Panvini, Le Rime, p. 231.

93   a) Contini, Li Origini, vol. 2:1, p. 775.
      b) Panvini, Le Rime, p. 471.
      c) Panvini, Le Rime, p. 423.

94   Contini, vol. 1, p. 250.
95   a) Contini, p. 736.
     b) Contini, p. 436.
     c) Contini, p. 442.
96   Contini, p. 784.
97   Contini, p. 770.
98   Panvini, Le Rime, p. 535.
99   Contini, vol. 2, p. 373.
100 Contini, p. 177.
101 Carducci, Antica Lirica Italiana, p. 12.
102 Carducci, ALA, p. 11.
103 Panvini, Le Rime, p. 480.
104 Contini, p. 355.
105 Contini, p. 555.

Chapter 4

> We may call this ethical criticism, interpreting ethics not as a rhetorical comparison of social facts to predetermined values, but as the consciousness of the presence of society. As a critical category this would be the sense of the real presence of culture in the community.
>
> Northrup Frye, <u>Anatomy</u> <u>of</u> <u>Criticism</u>

> However slight the terrestrial intercourse between Dante and Beatrice or Petrarch and Laura, time changes the proportion of things and in later days it is preferable to have fewer sonnets and more conversation.
>
> Marian Evans, <u>Middlemarch</u>

THE CULTURAL ECCENTRICITY OF THE FEMALE SPEAKER

Dramatic <u>personae</u> in the female voice in early Romance lyric are differentiated, as we saw in Chapter Three, at the level of roles. Poets found characters in their environment and in literary convention that could be recognized by their audiences. We have observed old-fashioned mothers and daughters whose love ethos is from an earlier time (Northern France); young court entertainers, probably Christian slave girls in Andalusia (Spain); saucy rural peasantry (Occitania); anxious village girls dependant on mothers, companions, and lovers for help with their problems of absence and parting (Portugal); and young daughters begging their parents to choose a husband (Italy). The surface diversity of type and situation disappears when we analyze the female <u>personae</u> by some general measures of social relationship. When studied in context, the female speaker in medieval lyric is seen to be, like her modern sister Eliza Doolittle, an embodiment of cultural inferiority in class status, social attitude, and language use. The inhabitant of marginal areas of society, the female speaker brings unity to the social picture in her function of complementary voice. She serves as a channel for pathos, dissent, irony, and humor. The vital role of the female voice is to remind us of the other side of things, the <u>eccentric</u> places in the social fabric. In this position, the young woman is a perpetual adolescent, engaged in battle with the grown-up world. Representative of both the juvenile and archaic values, her voice is the foil against which the centrist male voice is created and recognized.

But it is not sufficient, for a full interpretation of the female voice in medieval Romance lyric, to be able to describe the complementary role of the female _persona_. We must question the cultural environment in which this poetic phenomenon occurs. We may rightly suspect that song style--that most sensitive indicator of social change--reflected and reinforced conditions of medieval life. Europe in the period of our study experienced a "vital revolution" of expanded trade and agricultural production. The growing complexity of verbal procedures used by secular and religious institutions required a vernacular speech style suitable for courtly life and larger units of administration; a style characterized by restraint, elaboration of cause and effect, and elegant praise. This voice is identified in courtly lyric as male and aristocratic. The _chanson de femme_, on the other hand, which in less stratified, more egalitarian cultures accompanies work and ritual activities of the woman's group, became, as "borrowed" speech within troubadour lyrics, newly archaic, folkloric, and "popularisant." In this chapter we will illustrate the consistent marginality and cultural inferiority of the female speaker, using the measures of economic status, social attitude, and language use. With these thoughts and reflections, we prepare the way for our final chapter on the existence in Occitania of a number of women poets, the _trobairitz_. The work of this chapter, however, is to integrate the findings of Chapters 1, 2, and 3 into the economic and social conditions of medieval life.

The three measures, class status, social attitude, and language use, cannot be neatly separated from each other. Rather they form a thematic network of characteristics which determine the cultural importance of the female speaker. Poets draw on one or another of the characteristics for emphasis, or blend them all together for a fuller portrait. Their choices are determined by the need to illuminate a particular cultural question in song. If the poet's song illustrates the beauty of courtly language, the female speaker will speak in an outlandish dialect. For a contrast of class status, the poet will label the female speaker a _vilana_ or country woman. If he wants to highlight the _celar_, or hidden aspect of _fin'amor_, the female speaker will speak _apertamen_ in her use of open eroticism. To draw attention to the newer love ethos of male humility and female dominance, he will use for contrast an archaic _chanson de toile_, in which ladies pine and sigh for a rough military man. Thus we should not consider these three thematic characteristics as quantities found in separation but as qualities with which the poet can structure his cultural messages.

The female speaker is marked as a marginal or eccentric person by membership in a subordinate social and economic class. She may be a conquered slave girl, as in the _harǧa_.

a shepherdess as in the pastourelle, a feudal lady as in the chanson de toile, a village girl as in cantigas de amigo; surface differences only reinforce the remarkable consistency of her membership in a class that has no power at court. Her class has various origins and futures in medieval society, but in each case the poet takes pains to mark her class as other than aristocratic. He does this in several ways; by direct naming of her class, by a comic physical appearance, and by typified behavior.

Direct naming of a class appears in a widely used and longlived genre, the pastorela. Marcabru's seminal lyric "L'autrier jost' una sebissa" repeats the epithet vilana (country woman) in the center of each stanza of its twelve stanzas of coblas doblas (two stanzas with a matching rhyme) in the pattern AAABAAB. The female speaker's class designation is the key word of the lyric. It draws attention to the opposition of economic class and the distinction of the cultural semantic polarity cortezia-vilania:

> L'autrier jost' una sebissa
> Trobei pastora mestissa,
> De joi e de sen massissa,
> Si cum filla de vilana,
> Cap'e gonel'e pelissa
> Vest e camiza treslissa,
> Sotlars e caussas de lana.
>
> Ves lieis vinc per la planissa:
> "Toza, fi·m ieu, res faitissa,
> Dol ai car lo freitz vos fissa."
> --"Seigner, so·m dis la vilana,
> Merce Dieu e ma noirissa,
> Pauc m'o pretz si·l vens m'erissa,
> Qu'alegreta sui e sana."
>
> --"Toza, fi·m ieu, cauza pia,
> Destors me sui de la via
> Per far a vos compaignia;
> Quar aitals toza vilana
> No deu ses pareill paria
> Pastorgar tanta bestia
> En aital terra, soldana."
>
> --"Don, fetz ela, qui q·e m sia,
> Ben conosc sen e folia;
> La vostra pareillaria,
> Seigner, so·m dis la vilana,
> Lai on se tang si s'estia,
> Que tals la cuid' en bailia
> Tener, no·n a mas l'ufana."

--Toza de gentil afaire,
Cavaliers fon vostre paire
Que·us engenret en la maire,
Car fon corteza vilana.
Con plus vos gart, m'etz belaire,
E per vostre joi m'esclaire,
Si·m fossetz un pauc humana!"

--"Don, tot mon ling e mon aire
Vei revertir e retraire
Al vezoig et a l'araire,
Seigner, so·m dis la vilana;
Mas tals se fai cavalgaire
C'atrestal deuria faire
Los seis jorns de la setmana."

--"Toza, fi·m ieu, gentils fada,
Vos adastret, quan fos nada,
D'una beutat esmerada
Sobre tot' autra vilana;
E seria·us ben doblada,
Si·m vezi' una vegada,
Sobira e vos sotrana."

--"Seigner, tan m'avetz lauzada,
Que tota·n sui enojada;
Pois en pretz m'avetz levada,
Seigner, so·m dis la vilana,
Per so n'auretz per soudada
Al partir: bada, fols, bada,
E la muz'a meliana."

--"Toz', estraing cor e salvatge
Adomesg' om per uzatge.
Ben conosc al trespassatge
Qu'ab aital toza vilana
Pot hom far ric compaignatge
Ab amistat de coratge,
Si l'us l'autre non engana."

--"Don, hom coitatz de follatge
Jur' e pliu e promet gatge:
Si·m fariatz homenatge,
Seigner, so·m dis la vilana:
Mas ieu, per un pauc d'intratge
Non vuoil ges mon piucellatge,
Camjar per nom de putana."

--"Toza, tota creatura
Revertis a sa natura:
Pareillar pareilladura
Devem, ieu e vos, vilana,

> A l'abric lonc la pastura,
> Car plus n'estaretz segura
> Per far la cauza doussana."
>
> --"Don, oc; mas segon dreitura
> Cerca fols sa follatura,
> Cortes cortez' aventura,
> E il vilans ab la vilana;
> En tal loc fai sens fraitura
> On hom non garda mezura,
> So ditz la gens anciana."
>
> --"Toza, de vostra figura
> Non vi autra plus tafura
> Ni de son cor plus trefana."
>
> --"Don, lo cavecs vos ahura,
> Que tals bad' en la peintura
> Qu'autre n'espera la mana."[1]

Five of the twelve lines in which the class name *vilana* appears are identical: they are the address of the female speaker to the male whose pretentions to aristocratic status are comic. She says "Seignor" to him, honoring his assumed rank as a person of authority and dominant position while she is categorized as a person of low economic status. As we have noted before, it is important to keep in mind that the male is speaking throughout, reporting her speech. This central line in each stanza acts in a way reminiscent of a refrain, coming at the beginning of her speech in alternate stanzas. It establishes a mock inequality between the speakers, because she is patently his intellectual superior. Other signs of class distinction are present. Birth, source of either *cortezia* or *vilania,* further defines the female speaker. She is called the daughter of a peasant woman, rather than the daughter of a man, suggesting commonness or uncertain parentage. The epithet *toza* marks her as a lower class woman (der. *tonsa,* girl) in contrast to the word *donsela* or *donzelha* (der. *dominicella,* maiden, young lady). Stanza five refers again to the mother, in ironic contrast of courtly and rustic. In a clumsy attempt to seduce by flattery, the male *persona* calls the girl's mother a *corteza vilana,* an oxymoronic term that again emphasizes the lyric's theme, the distance between the classes of society.

The class status of the female speaker in succeeding *pastorelas* is revealed in the occupation she follows: she is a rural *pastora* herding sheep or goats. In the Castilian *serranilla,* she is a mountain dweller, a fierce, dark-skinned *mestissa*, a dirty, fat swine-maiden, dark as pitch. In the French corpus, she is pretty, *de gent cors, fresche et colore*, and in a lyric of the Portuguese King Dinis she is *Ua pastor ben talhada*. A *pastourelle* of the Italian poet

Ciacco Dall'Anguillara begins with the knight's address and description of the lady:

> "O gemma leziosa
> adorna villanella . . ."

to which she replies tartly:

> "Assai son gemme in terra
> ed in fiume ed in mare
> e' hanno vertute in guerra
> e fanno altra' alegrare.
> Amico, io non son essa
> di quelle tre nessuna
> altrove va'per essa
> e cerca altra persona." [2]

Her location at a distance from the court is noted in the opening word of many of these conventional lyrics, L'autrier or Noutro dia, phrases which indicate to the audience that it was not here at court, but out there in the country where the courtly speaking male meets the speaking woman.

The use of the female voice for contrast in the area of class status: senher/vilana, cortezia/vilania, may also be found in the female speaker's social attitudes. Several thematic oppositions can be named, of which the female voice expresses one pole: celadamen/apertamen (secretly/ openly or frankly); felonia/merci, pensar/esbaudir, greu/leu; folatge/ mezura. Similarly, in facing the large social institutions of medieval culture (marriage, the church, the king, crusades, monastic life) the female voice can be a vehicle for expression of heterodox attitudes with impunity for the poet. She may lament, protest, complain, and even blaspheme publicly against the most sacred icons, but her expression lacks potency because it is in the voice of the "other," not the generic "self" in Sartrean terms. The female voice thus serves as a vent for dissatisfaction without creating a pressure to redress the power of the individual over the institution. It is pathetic and harmless; a pleasing combination of emotions which allows the audience to empathize without the threat of a call to action. She (the female speaker) is veiled in anonymity and cannot therefore be responsible for a specific charge of heterodoxy. A non-person in legal codes, the ward or charge of men, she has a freedom of dissent like the fool, and can give voice to the frustrations felt by the whole population.

One of the tenets of fin'amor is secrecy, but the female speaker typically makes an open avowal of her love. Jonathan Saville observes that the female speaker in the alba, the dawn love song, is more passionate than the knight, and more eloquent in her expression of feeling. Her joy in the pleasure of love is more intense, as is her grief at the separation. She loves only for love, and is the chief upholder of the erotic values of the inner world, having no real existence anywhere else. One of the characteristic rhetorical devices of the <u>alba</u>, the use of an optative subjunctive, is associated with her speech pattern. as "Plagues a Dieu ja la nueitz non falhis."[3] Of the three characters in the drama of the <u>alba</u>, the lady rejects the outer reality of the world, the knight rejects it then accepts it, and the watchman accepts it from the very beginning. The ecstatic, erotic voice of the speaker of the Mozarabic ḫarǧa has been noted in earlier chapters, but we will mention again only her direct love call:

> 0 my seducer, come here when
> the tasks of war release you.   (Sola Solé 46)

her explicit command:

> You will not see me except on condition
> That you join my ankle bracelets to my earrings.
>   (Sola Solé 48)

and her admission of the force of her love:

> This shameless man, mother, this madman attacks me
> with force, and we are lost in his ocean wave.
> (Sola Solé 49)

The unstudied, spontaneous tone of her <u>cri du coeur</u> is a counterpoint that highlights the male voice rhetoric of elaboration and hyperbole.

"Quant se vient en mai ke rose est panie" is a nun's complaint in the metric scheme of ten syllable lines rhyming aaab BB in the female voice style. It is in the frame pattern with a male narrator opening and closing the lyric, although each stanza is followed by a refrain in a female voice. God, Jesus, and the Virgin Mary are invoked for help in freeing the nun from the convent, as we see in stanza two:

> Ki nonne me fist, Jesus lou maldie!
> Je di trop envis vespres ne complies;
> car asseiz aing miels bonne compaingnie,
> ke est deduissans et amerouseste.
>   Je sant les douls mals leis ma centurete
>   malois soit de Deu ki me fist nonnete!

and the Virgin will help her escape with her lover, "Maix ieu en istrai, per Sainte Marie", [4] and they will seek the good life in Paris. Although the lyric is a two-part poem with a masculine voice frame, the female voice carries the message of complaint about religious restrictions on sexual desire. The verbal artifacts of medieval culture presented women as more lascivious than men, and the lyric lends itself to a comic, mock-pathetic treatment.

Not only the religious, but also the secular rulers were objects for protest in the female voice. In the <u>cantigas de amigo</u> particularly we find many lyrics in which the young woman complains that the king has taken away her lover. Two of these are in conversations with a female friend. From the repertoire of King Dinis himself:

> Amiga, muit'á gran sazon
> que se foi d'aqui con el-rei
> meu amigo, mais já cuidei
> mil vezes no meu coraçon.   (Nunes 5)

Similarly, in a lyric of D. Fernan Fernandez Cogominho:

> Amiga, muit'á que non sei,
> nen mi ar veestes vós dizer
> novas, que querria saber,
> dos que ora son con el-rei:
> > se se veen ou se x'estam
> > ou a que tempo se verram   (Nunes 136)

In stanza two she wants news of "dos que el-rei levou sigo:" and in the third she would be grateful for news "del-rei e dos que con el son:" Symbols of the king's power, his ships also cause distress. A group of <u>barcarolas</u> in the <u>leixa-pren</u> (drop and pick up) technique of interlacing lines expresses the thought of the <u>amiga</u>'s loss:

> Vi eu, mia madr', andar
> as barcas eno mar:
> > e moiro-me d'amor.   (Nunes 79)

Or the mother informs the daughter of the ship's arrival, in a lyric of Juan Bolseiro:

> Filha fremosa, por vos non mentir,
> vej'eu as barcas pelo mar viir
> > en que se foi voss'amigo d'aqui.   (Nunes 398)

The <u>amiga</u> often takes a position on the event of her lover's going to join the king's army. She may go to follow him, a motif found in other Romance women's songs. In a lyric of Gonçalo Eanes do Vinhal, she invokes the help of God as a higher power than the king, his subject:

>   Sei eu, donas, que deitad'é d'aqui
>   do reino ja meu amigu'e non sei
>   como lhi vai, mais quer'ir a el-rei,
>   chorar-lh'ei muito e direi lh'assi:
>   por Deus, senhor, que vos tan bon rei fez
>   perdoad'a meu amigu'esta vez.   (Nunes 146)

Or she may be resigned to his departure, and ask news of him:

>   Amigo, queredes-vos ir?
>   e ben sei eu que mi averra:
>   em mentre morardes ala,
>   a quantos end'eu vir viir
>   a todos eu preguntarei
>   como vos vai en cas d'el-rei.   (Nunes 319)

She may go to the shore and wait for him:

>   Jus'a lo mar é o rio:
>   eu, namorada, irei
>   u el-rei arma navio;
>   Amores, convusco m'irei.   (Nunes 388)

She may be willing to sacrifice her life, serving him further to the extent of withholding the reason for her death:

>   Foi-s'o meu amigo a cas d'el-rei
>   e, amigas, con grand'amor que lh'ei,
>   quand'el veer, ja eu morta serei,
>   mais non lhe digan que morri assi,
>   ça, se souber com'eu por el morri,
>   sera mui pouca sa vida des i.(Nunes 320)

There may be the inducement of gifts from afar, which she, however, refuses. A girlfriend talks to the *délaissée*:

>   --O voss'amigo, que s'a cas del-rei
>   foi, amiga, mui cedo vos verra
>   e partide ben doas que vos dara
>   --Amiga, verdade ben vos direi:
>   fara-mi Deus ben, se mi-o adusser
>   e sas doas dê-as a quen quiser. (Nunes 317)

On a sinister note, the girl may become a gift for the king. A mother-daughter dialogue shows a confused maiden and a mother who takes the king's part:

> --Cabelos, los meus cabelos,
> el-rei m'enviou por elos;
> madre, que lhis farei?
> --Filha, dade-os a el-rei.   (Nunes 385)

Here the king is seen as more than a threat to love; he is a threat to the young woman herself. The mother advises a submission to the king's authority. Although the king is typically the agent of separation and thus a cause of distress, in one lyric he restores her lover:

> Disseron-m'oj', ai amiga, que non
> é meu amig'almirante do mar
> e meu coraçon ja pode folgar.   (Nunes 221)

She catalogues all the troubles she will no longer have now that her lover is returned from the frontier. Kathleen Ashley, writing of the emotional world of the *amiga*, discounts the usual critical view that the female voice in Galician-Portuguese lyrics expresses "an intense and uncomplicated yearning for her absent loved one," and claims instead:

> . . . these poems evoke the complex emotional states of the *amiga*, whose voice issues from a dynamic universe of arrivals and departures, reports and rumors, shared joy, or the menace of uncertainty, misperception, and even betrayal . . . [5]

Many songs explicitly blame the king and his activity for the *amiga*'s anxiety and distress. Those songs create an assumption of blame in other songs where the lover has left home for an unspecified location. It is a universal phenomenon that the creation of a level of government superior to the local level means the disruption of matrilocal village life, as males move away for military service or economic advantage. The obsessive tone of anxiety about the lover and the debates on points of etiquette about taking him back or allowing him to leave show that the poet used the female voice to express a varied response to the claims of the courts on the population.

The theme of lament directed against both the secular king and the king of heaven that we saw in Gonçalo Eanes do Vinhal's lyric, is found in an earlier poem, Marcabru's "A la fontana del vergier." The female speaker, within a male-voice frame structures laments the absence of her lover, blaming in turn Jesus reys del mon, as well as King Louis VII and God for the deprivation of her happiness. Finally, in a rational turn of thought characteristic of the female voice in Provençal, she dismisses the prospect of joy in a future heaven, and concludes on a note of philosophical resignation:

> . . . mas pauc me te
> Que trop s'es de mi alonhatz.

which has been interpreted as a blame placed on the lover himself who cared too little for her to remain with her.[6]

Considering the complaints of the female voice about king and court from a greater level of abstraction, we can say that the problem they express is power/impotence. The woman who laments has very little power to influence the forces that are changing her life. She therefore explores the possible positions that the weak in any stratified culture have available to them: protest, lament, petition, withholding support, and non-cooperation. She can blame rather than praise the figure who is publicly applauded and sustained in power by force. In these lyrics, the female voice expresses the dissent of individuals with social power. The intellectual physiognomy that we look for in a dramatic characterization consists of a response to the challenge of powerlessness. But the voice of blame is the voice of comedy, and the literary presentation of frustrated desire easily crosses the line from pathos to laughter.

The song of protest and complaint about marriage, a genre called the malmariée, flourished in Northern France and can be found, though in fewer examples, in other Romance literatures. The tone of the female voice is frequently rebellious and hostile, as in the following lyric:

> Soufrés, maris, et si ne vous anuit:
> Demain m'arés et mes amis anuit.
> Je vous deffenc k'un seul mot n'en parlés:
> Soufrés maris, et si ne vous mouvés.
> La nuit est courte, aparmains me rarés,
> Quant mes amis ara fait sen deduit.
> Soufrés, maris, et si ne vous anuit:
> Demain m'arés et mes amis anuit.[7]

The songs are often in rondo form, and generally anonymous. Critics have offered numerous explanations for the appearance and popularity of this song. Jeanroy thought they were "pure convention" and "monstreux si on les prenait au sérieux."[8] In his book devoted to the genre, Rudolf Dähne could not account for the subject matter. Bédier, Gaston Paris, and Jeanroy linked the songs to May Day songs of the pre-courtly period, and tried to settle on a particular region of France, either the South proper, or the border area of Poitou and Limousin. However, the schematic nature of the song and the structurally important but shadowy presentation of the lover, as well as the frequency and persistent life of this genre suggest that it is related to the many "wedding songs" that tease the groom and his family. In traditional village society, these songs are sung by the companions of the young bride who will leave the security of her family to assume the risks of marriage and child bearing. Musical anthropologists have documented many of these songs in other areas, telling us that they are typically a part of the extended period of pre-marriage celebrations.[9] They function for the women's group as a cultural protection and instruction, in the same way that the boasting song does for the men's group. In this sense, the <u>malmariée</u> would be a counterpart of the <u>pastourelle</u>, both songs filling a cultural need for guidance, comfort, and encouragement in sexual roles.

The popularity of the <u>malmariée</u> in courtly lyric may be explained by the changes in the institution of marriage. During the period of our study, the twelfth and thirteenth centuries, marriage became a bond more rigorously construed. Previously, mutual consent in two stages: first, <u>palabras</u> <u>de</u> <u>futur</u> or engagement, followed at an indeterminate interval by <u>palabras</u> <u>de</u> <u>presente</u>, marriage, and these words spoken by the couple were enough to establish the legality of family cohabitation. As the Roman Church assumed secular power, it arrogated to itself authority over civil marriage. It placed more effective stress on the eternal and spiritual nature of the sacrament of marriage. Two witnesses and church registration became a requirement for legal marriage under penalty of religious sanctions.[10] Written documents binding the couple made marriage more difficult to dissolve. As pressure for acceptance of the indissolubility of marriage grew, the "carnival" values of the marriage protest song gained importance.

Speech style is probably the most important element of dramatic characterization in a work of literature. Speech encodes information about our occupation, our sex, our social status, economic class and political position as a member of a ruling group, a dominated group, or an isolated group. The troubadour had available to him a range of possibilities for speech style in drawing the character of the female speaker. He used many of them, in addition to the general features of female speech that have been identified by linguists. It is a key element in the female voice that the female character speak in an identifiably different manner from the male. The "otherness" of her speech, however, cannot be total, or her speech would be incomprehensible to the audience and lose all semantic value. The poet, therefore, must choose a speech that is part way between the male courtly style and a totally foreign speech. He must find in his environment a style that will answer the need for a separate category of speech intelligible to his audience. Medieval Romance poets solved the problem in different ways in each Romance language, but the strategy of their solutions is identical: the poet measured a distance from female speech to male speech.

In the speech environment in which two cultures co-exist, the female speaks in the style of the superseded or dominated group. The Mozarabic woman's song in the Arabic muwashsha illustrates the principle. A few token words were sufficient to tag the female speaker as a member of the Mozarabic-speaking sub-culture. In ḫarǧa 51, for example, two Romance words mamma and so give an exotic flavor to the girl's song:

> Mamma, ay habibi,
> So'l jummella shaqrella,
> el collo albo
> e boquella hamrella.
>
> Mother, what a lover!
> Under the fair hair
> the white neck
> and rosy mouth!   (Sola Solé 51)

Often an Arabic word used in the ḫarǧa will have a Romance diminutive or ending. Bilingualism is characteristic of the ḫarǧas.

Similarly, the female speaker in Raimbaut de Vaqueiras' "Domna, tant vos ai pregada" speaks not in a totally incomprehensible foreign tongue, but in a dialect, Genoese, which lacks the literary prestige of the male speaker's Provençal. The transition from one speech to the other is thus not a complete break, but a shift of linguistic perspective

from his,   e pois serai meills pagatz
            que s'era mia'l ciutatz
            ab l'aver qu'es aiostatz
                dels Genoes.

to her,   Iuair, voi no se' corteso
            qi me chaideiai de zò,
            que negota no·n faro[11]

Both voices use the aab rhyme pattern typical of the female voice, but the use of dialect underscores her comic realism and his comic aristocratic idealism. As well as the aspiration for love, there is the failure of aspiration, the deflation of a dream.

Cross-cultural and dialectal speech was not the only resource for the poet needing a linguistic contrast for male/female speech distinctions. Archaic speech representing a culturally outdated love ethic provided vivid illumination to the newer courtly style. French <u>chansons de toile</u> were employed for a brief period to define by contrast the changing requirements for men and women in society. These songs show women waiting for an absent warrior who pursues military goals with little thought of courtly graces. As Michel Zink writes:

> . . . ces filles de roi ou d'empereur aiment des guerriers professionnels, des baroudeurs, des mercenaires, des <u>soudoiers</u> <u>d'autre</u> <u>terre</u>, venus d'ailleurs, attirés par un tournoi ou par une guerre, prêts a partir ailleurs, et qui, au mieux, les emmèneront bien loin, <u>en leur contree</u>.[12]

Dialogue in the <u>chanson de toile</u> is typically between a mother and her daughter. Sitting in a chamber sewing, the mother discovers an unhappy young woman unable to spin. She may help her daughter to marry, "Bele Aiglentine, vos prendra il Henris?" or scold her, "Chastoi vos en, Bele Yolanz." In one song the mother prevails upon her husband to consent to the daughter's choice of husband:

> Sor sa meire Amelot se pamait
> deus, keil pitiet la meire a cuer en ait!
> tout an plorant doucemant la basait
> a redresier trop bien la confortait.
>
> La meire vit son enfant angossous.
> trop bial li dist 'fille, rahaitiez vos.
> Garin ameis, si l'averes a spous
> se m'aist deus, il est vaillans et prous.[13]

The genuineness of archaic language in the <u>chansons de toile</u> has been challenged and discussed by critics.[14] The question of authenticity only corroborates the rhetorical argument because the poet may well have striven for the <u>effect</u> of archaic speech while building on the model of a genuinely archaic song, as Paul Zumthor shows in his study of "Bele Aiglentine." The paratactic style of the second line,

> En un vergier lez une fontenele
> dont clere est l'onde et blanche la gravele,[15]

and the epic vocabulary of

> Bele Doette les degrez en avale[16]

serve to recall to the audience the sounds of an earlier time. Archaic speech and modified archaic speech invite comparison to the modernity of the courtly style and manner.

Not only in the Old French chansons de toile but throughout medieval courtly lyric, the quality of archaism pervades the female voice. As we saw in Chapter Two, the female speaker typically employs repetition and nonsense speech, styles which place her voice close to what Andrew Welsh calls "the roots of lyric." The refrain, primary exclamations, incantation and nonsense words, characteristic of female speech, are backward-looking devices from which the poet must detach the male voice for the rational tone he was creating in the vernacular lyric. Refrains, by their association with communal singing, evoke a previous state of society in which the group had precedence over the individual self. They often express musical notes if the pastora is playing an instrument or weeping over her misfortune:

> civalala duri duriaus
> civalala durete [17]
>
> et dit 'e, ae! o, or ae!
> bien m'ont amors desfie. [18]

The incantatory style, still audible in medieval female speech, is an archaizing expressive style which drops away from the male voice in the literary song, although it never disappeared from Iberian popular lyric. Incantation is a musical style appropriate to a culture that holds a belief in the unity of all life, whereas the densely verbal male-voice style of new material in each line of verse accompanies a culture that separates secular and sacred, and whose institutions of education, government, and religion are male-dominated.

We have seen that the female speaker, in spite of differences of roles in the separate Romance literatures, uniformly occupies a complementary position of cultural inferiority to the male speaker. She may represent a conquered race, a superseded class, a low occupational rank; she laments and protests her losses caused by king and church; her speech is frequently archaic, erotic, primitive, incantatory. The contrast of male and female speech style can be seen at another level of analysis when it is viewed from the perspective of classical theory of rhetoric: ethos, logos, and pathos. A dramatic mask, or persona, must be a recognizable individual and at the same time express deeply rooted human attitudes.[19] Its ability to remain stable gives it the power of a cultural value through repeated performances.

In the polyphony of medieval dramatic lyric, the female voice remains stable because it is rooted in a basic triadic relationship. Three complementary voices structure the system of rhetoric: ethos, logos. and pathos. The triad of relationships consists of, 1) a feeling self. whose mode of cognition and experience is emotion (pathos), 2) a conscious self. whose mode of knowing and experiencing is reason (logos), and 3) an environmental entity, whose mode of cognition and experience is more general and presses the two others into relevence with the whole, it is intuition. Language contains the triadic structure of relationships in its first, second. and third persons, the subjective "I," the "other," "you"; and the objective "he, she, or it." In Figure 2, the triad may be seen with the communication pattern indicated by directional arrows. As the male poet in courtly lyric reserves for the male persona the most conscious, hence archetypal voice, he uses the female persona as a convenient strategy for expression of the complementary or subdominant voice. The division is not exclusive; as we saw with formal patterns of lyric, the male voice may also occupy the sub-dominant place in themes that are counterparts to the archetypal theme.

Figure 2

Triad of Male/Female Voice Relationship
in Medieval Romance Courtly Lyric

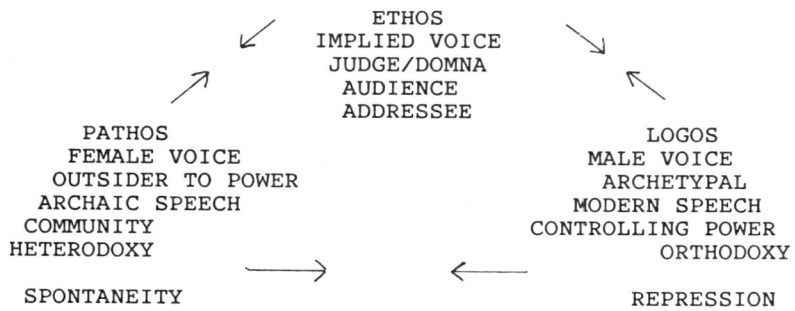

A lyric poem may be seen as a locus of conflict in which the subjective, mixed, and objective views described above meet. In this theoretical view, the human communication pattern is a talking person, talking with someone about a third thing or person. Experience reflected in lyric poetry contains these three relations, stretched out over the range of poet/text/listener, or held within the poem as poet/persona/object.[19] The female presence becomes a useful strategy with which the poet can mark one corner of the triangle. The female persona's speech functions as a symbol of "otherness." By virtue of women's genuine otherness from males in appearance, experience, and attitude, the female voice is a sign for a quality of difference. In medieval Romance lyric, the speaking woman often plays the dramatic role of the first person, pathos. She is typically imaged as the feeling element, primitive desire, or as a speaker for the opposition to established order in the arena of the poem. Her voice appears in such a way--close juxtaposition--that the terms of the conflict will stand in sharp relief.

But it is essential that we translate the psychological polarity logos/pathos of male/female voice relationship into the socio-economic perspective of medieval culture. The assignment of a pathetic and archaizing tone to female speech serves a specific rhetorical purpose in the linguistic environment of the rising aristocratic class. For his courtly audience, the vernacular poet must define the logos-oriented male voice by the use of a contrastive voice. Under this cultural constraint, the male poet commissions the female voice to carry the "other" part of the psyche, the archaic and pathetic tones. Female speech is fragmented and incorporated within a dominant male voice only under the conditions of a particular pattern of culture: the emergence of a complex, stratified and male-dominant power hegemony. The female voice in lyric poetry of less hierarchical and more evenly balanced cultures has been gathered by folklorists and anthropologists in primitive and traditional societies around the world. Willard Trask's *The Unwritten Song* shows us, among other collections, hundreds of examples of songs that belong to the women's group alone.[21] They reveal the concerns of the women's group for protection and preservation of human life. Their songs mark the stages of human development from birth to puberty to courtship and marriage, old age and death. In communal songs, women participate in social life, performing ritual tasks essential to the community. Their songs encourage and celebrate the successful passage of life's stages, and teach the social attitudes appropriate to their own culture, giving a rhythmic background for each day's activity. We can accept the evidence from musical anthropologists and their song collections that women employ a body of song that belongs to their cultural life at the lower levels of economic subsistence. These songs function independently of the men's group songs and whole group songs.

The anonymous "Trois sereurs seur rive mer" from the Old French corpus illustrates the teaching function of songs in the traditional style. Line repetitions, rondo dance form, and symbolic elements of number (three) and natural objects (river bank, tree branch) reinforce a message of wisdom in love relations:

> Trois sereurs seur rive mer
> chantent cler:
> "la jonete fu brunete:
> de brun ami j'aati,
> je sui brune,
> s'avrai brun ami ausi."
>
> Trois sereurs seur rive mer
> chantent cler:
> la mainnee apele
> Robin son ami:
> "prise m'avez el bois ramé,
> reportez m'i."
>
> Trois sereurs seur rive mer
> chantent cler:
> l'ainee dit:
> "on doit bien jone dame amer
> et s'amour garder
> cil qui l'a." [22]

The three sisters singing on a river bank (a familiar motif in European folksong) introduce a theme in a step-by-step sequence. The youngest begins the lesson: a man who is similar to her will apeal to her. The middle sister already has a lover, and accepts his gift, while the oldest sister is concerned with the retention of love. The extreme patterning provides, with folkloric economy and intensity, an entire instruction on the course of love: how to choose, receive the gift, and the importance of keeping it. This miniature guide book teaches women who are all three sisters in the progress of a lifetime. The youngest, still at the choosing stage, needs a criterion for judgment, likeness; the middle sister gets the terms of her dialogue with Robin clear, and learns to receive, and the oldest, concerned with holding love, speaks of the problem of loyalty.

The symbolic visual imagery of the song lifts the message out of a prosaic didactic style into an imaginary and mythic world. Women's songs often use the appeal of symbolic objects and numbers. The object or number cannot, however, be interpreted as corresponding to a single meaning in a linear pattern. Resonance, rather than equivalence, dominates the symbolic mode. Its power comes from its ability to translate emotional states within which opposite feelings coexist into a pleasurable language which is no less true than that of descriptive logic.[23] The language of symbols is strongly social, and its use in women's songs creates a powerful artistic expression.[24]

In the early medieval centuries, the oral culture of vernacular speech would require women's songs to accompany work, to celebrate rituals and festivals, and to provide social learning for younger members of the group in songs such as "Trois sereurs seur rive mer." Men were principally warriors in a military/agricultural society; women worked as managers, manufacturers, and producers of essential goods in a home-centered socio-economic structure. The working life of women in pre-capitalist organization of production was recognized by Karl Marx. In his introduction to the English translation of <u>Formen</u> <u>der</u> <u>die</u> <u>Kapitalistischen</u> <u>Produktion</u> <u>vorhergehen</u> (<u>Pre-Capitalist</u> <u>Economic</u> <u>Formations</u>), Eric J. Hobsbawm quotes Marx:

> Every individual household contains an entire economy, forming as it does an independent center of production (<u>manufacture</u> <u>merely</u> <u>the</u> <u>domestic</u> <u>subsidiary</u> <u>labour</u> <u>of</u> <u>the</u> <u>women</u>) (emphasis added).[25]

There is a <u>consensus</u> <u>gentium</u> that women in a village or manorial society have a greater share of power in a community than they do when higher governmental structures draw power from groups of villages. The cause of this phenomenon is attributed by various thinkers to a number of factors. Simone de Beauvoir claims that when men gain control over the judicial system or courts they legislate the depowering of women in such areas as inheritance rights, ownership of land, and control of children. Joseph Campbell sees the "takeover" in terms of myth, and has no answer to why Ishtar, for instance, becomes the "abomination" of the book of Genesis, or why Athena and Lakshmi at about the same time in history become absorbed by the male deity. In his analysis of song style and culture, Alan Lomax affirms that song style changes in relation to the number of governmental levels above the local. With four political levels (local, county, state, and national) song texts become "textheavy" with new material in each line, fewer repetitions and male speech dominance.[26] It seems clear that the independence or subordination of the female voice to the male voice in song style is directly correlated to the socio-economic framework of a given culture.

The altered relation of women to music in courtly and urban life results from individualizing or "privatizing" of women, as feminists say. We are familiar with the dictum that a sense of individuality comes with the change from manorial or feudal society to the castle/town, as the rules of competition replace cooperation and that the new sense of individuality is evident in medieval Romance courtly lyric and narrative.

When manufacture passes from the home to urban work centers and when concomitant trade and banking require men to travel for sales and purchasing, the place of women in society changes. Her power may be called "actual" in the small area of the village, and "symbolic" in the centralized court/towns. After 1200, with the increase of urban wealth, women began to assume a conspicuous consumption role, displaying the signs of rank in richly ornamented costumes with exaggerated lines and imposing headdresses. Eunice Goddard, in her study of the vocabulary of dress in early medieval French literature, points out that women's clothing changed radically as her dress evolved from the loose garments of the sexually neutral type to the fitted gowns worn by wealthy women in the later medieval period.[27] Manuscript illustrations document the change of style for clothing and house architecture.

Also during this period the flow of dowry money reversed its direction. A chronic scarcity of women, which had existed since ancient times, began to change as longevity rates for women altered, giving them a few more years.[28] There were now more women to be married than husbands to be found. A father had to dower his daughter if she were to attract a husband. Dante notes the spiraling cost of marriage in the contrast of older and newer conditions of marriage:

> Non faceva, nascendo, ancor paura
> la figlia al padre; che 'l tempo e la dote
> non fuggien quinci e quindi la misura.
> (<u>Paradiso</u> 15:103-5)

In the voice of Cacciaguida, Dante speaks of the social and economic changes that came with the flow of wealth and ensuing pressures on the fabric of human relations. Florence is a rich bourgeoise wearing the new items of finery, ". . . catenella, corona, gonne contigiate, cintura che fosse a veder piu che la persona." He visualizes the new isolation of a wife whose husband is trading at the fairs in France:

> O fortunate! ciascuna era certa
> della sua sepultura, ed ancor nulla era
> per Francia nel letto diserta. (<u>Paradiso</u> 15:118-120)

Even the linguistic importance of women in oral cultures is noted in the same speech; a mother's special role as story teller and teacher of history:

> L'altra, traendo alla rocca la chioma,
> favoleggiava con la sua famiglia
> de' Troiani, di Fiesole e di Roma.
> (Paradiso 15:121-123)

Dante writes of costly clothing, painted faces, and disrupted family life as signs of the new times. But evidence of a radical change in women's lives may be found in courtly lyric itself. The new style of fragmentation and incorporation of the female voice within courtly lyric articulated for the courtly world the transition from an outmoded song style to the new vernacular courtly style. Lyrics mediated the new consciousness. Mirroring the vision of women in canon law as Eva and Ave, the low and the high, courtly lyric style fulfilled a cultural need on the part of the new ruling group. It (the new class) could feel its power in regard to the older organization of society. Female members of superseded classes singing parts of songs from earlier periods are placed in a "one-step-down" position, enclosed by the new style of speech and behavior. In this way, courtly lyric contains a double image of the female; the dazzling view of a symbolically powerful domna, and her shadow, the erotic, uncouth, anxious, or unhappy woman of the lesser classes. Since speech is characteristic of the negatively-coded woman, silence is the positive value for the lady of the court. How it happens that a group of women poets emerged in Provençal, alone of all the Romance literatures, will be the subject of the following chapter.

In conclusion, we may well ask whether the study of the female voice in medieval courtly lyric has significance for our own time. The conventions of the female voice extend, as we saw in Chapter One, from at least Hellenistic poetry to the contemporary work of Robert Frost, W. B. Yeats and Thomas Hardy. Modern research shows two things about female speech in the history of poetry: 1) that women poets have contributed far more to the history of lyric poetry than was formerly known or collected for study, and 2) women's comparative silence is the result of cultural constraints. Much remains to be done before cultural stereotypes are exchanged for other, truer pictures. Women now see that as muteness is coded and learned, expression in public life can also be coded and learned. Each human being, male and female, is a source of claims, as religious and legal thought teaches; so each person, to achieve full humanity, must become, in the beautiful phrase of Mikhail Bakhtin, "an integrated center of speech, able to tolerate other speech without assimilating it to the core, and resisting assimilation into another person's speech.[29]

Notes to Chapter 4

1   Hill and Bergin, Anthology of the Provençal Troubadours, I, p. 20.

2   Carducci, Antica lirica italiana, p. 20.

3   Jonathan Saville, The Medieval Erotic Alba: Structure as Meaning (New York, 1972), p. 9.

4   Carla Cremonesi, La Lirica francese del medio evo (Milan: Verese, 1955), p. 67; Bec, La Lyrique française au moyen âge, vol. 2, p. 20.

5   Kathleen Ashley, "The Role of the Courts and the Thirteenth-Century Portuguese Lyric," ACTA 3 (1976), 65-78.

6   Anna Granville Hatcher, "Marcabru's 'A la fontana del vergier,' Modern Language Notes, 79 (1964), 284-95.

7   Bec, La Lyrique française au moyen âge, vol. 2, p. 16.

8   See Chapter Four, "La Chanson Dramatique," in Alfred Jeanroy, Les Origines de la poésie lyrique française, esp. pp. 85-89.

9   See Edward O. Henry, "North Indian Wedding Songs," Journal of South Asian Literature 11 (1975), 61-93.

10 A. H. Marques de Oliveira, A Sociedade medieval portuguesa: aspectos de vida quotidiana, Trans. S. S. Wyatt as Daily Life in Portugal in the Late Middle Ages.

11 Hill and Bergin, Anthology, vol. 1, p. 145.

12 Michel Zink, Belle: essai sur les chansons de toile: suivi d'une édition et d'une traduction, (Paris: Champion, 1978), p. 64.

13 Zink, Belle, pp. 102-104.

14 See the discussion and bibliography on this problem in Zink, Belle, pp. 66-71, and in Paul Zumthor, "La chanson de Bele Aiglentine," Travaux de Linguistique et de Littérature 8, 1, (1970) 325-337.

15 Zink, Belle, p. 85.

16 Zink, Belle, p. 90.

17 Karl Bartsch, Altfranzösische Romanzen und Pastourellen, p. 179.

[18] Bartsch, Rom. und Past., p. 72.

[19] George Wright, The Poet in the Poem, (Berkeley: Univ. of California Press, 1968), Chapter One.

[20] Wright, p. 20.

[21] Willard Trask, The Unwritten Song, 2 vols. (New York: Macmillan, 1958).

[22] Bec, La Lyrique, vol. 2, p. 45.

[23] Gaston Bachelard, Le Psychoanalyze du feu.

[24] See the Introduction to the Dictionnaire des Symboles, (Paris: UNESCO, 1968).

[25] Karl Marx, Pre-Capitalist Economic Formations, trans. Jack Cohen, (New York: International Publishers, 1965), p. 45.

[26] Alan Lomax, Folk Song Style and Culture, (Washington, D.C.: Association for the Advancement of Science, 1968).

[27] Eunice Goddard, Women's Costume in French Texts of the Eleventh and Twelfth Centuries. The Johns Hopkins Studies in Romance Literatures and Languages, vol. 7, 1927.

[28] David Herlihy, "The Medieval Marriage Market," in Medieval and Renaissance Studies 6 (Southeastern Institute of Medieval and Renaissance Studies, Proceedings, Summer, 1974) 1976.

[29] Mikhail Bakhtin, Problems of Dostoevsky's Poetics, p. 201.

Chapter 5

> Signs are small measurable things, but interpretations are illimitable.
> Marian Evans, <u>Middlemarch</u>

> . . . but beware of arriving at conclusions without comparison.
> Marian Evans, <u>Daniel Deronda</u>

THE TROBAIRITZ

As we begin to piece together the world history of women poets, to publish and study their work, we find that women poets flourished in courtly societies of the major cultures.[1] Those whose names and biographies have been recorded were sheltered by the protective institutions of court and convent. The release from physical labor that wealth and rank permitted, the demand for refinement and pleasure and the cultivation and patronage of the arts created an environment in which women poets found an audience. Noble women, courtesans. and religious have left a tradition of lyric, much of which is innovative in rhythms and theme. The homely lullabies, nursery songs, children's game songs and work songs of the Middle Ages, which girls learned and mothers taught, have largely been lost to us unless included as "borrowed speech" in a written form or preserved by clerical vagaries. Thus we have a Welsh lullaby in the manuscript of the epic <u>Gododdin</u>, a non-sequitur in the text, probably a marginal scribbling from an earlier copy.[2] But in the great courtly traditions of Tamil, Japanese (in Japan women wrote the first vernacular lyric because they were not permitted to learn Chinese, the official language of court poetry), Chinese, Urdu, Persian, Arabic, and Greek, women poets' names and works have been preserved. The Provençal <u>trobairitz</u> take their place in this history as an important but not a unique phenomenon.

Poetry by women has only just begun to be gathered and published in separate anthologies.[3] Poetry by medieval European women poets has not (1981) been collected and studied against the background of the corpus of lyric in that period, although such important poets as Marie de France, Hildegard von Bingen, and the Comtessa de Dia were contemporaries. Even the sketch of a synthetic treatment of medieval women's poetry is beyond the scope of the present chapter. Rather, in these pages, we shall attempt to answer questions concerning the female voice and its relation to the named women poets. Why did lyrics of twenty women poets survive in Provençal literature, but none or very few survive in other Romance languages? What are the qualities of this poetry? What is its relation to the function of the female voice in male-dominated lyric speech as it has been here described? How did women poets respond to the conventions of the female speech model they were surrounded by? If, as Bakhtin suggests, the heroic task is to find a "reciprocal" speech that neither blankets other speech nor is invaded by other speech, how did women in Occitania achieve an individual voice, a place in the social dialogue?[4] Did they reverse the terms of courtly love, as Jeanroy thought and Ferrante agrees? Did they fail to achieve a voice, as Shapiro believes? How were they imitative, and how innovative? We will first review the small corpus as background for a discussion of these problems.

Some twenty manuscripts, mostly copied in Italy, preserve the lyrics of the *trobairitz*. Two of them contain illuminations of Castelloza of Auvergne and the Comtessa de Dia. The date of the earliest extant lyric by a woman in Provençal, "Bels dous amics . . ." of Tibors, ca. 1150, was established by Walter T. Pattison in his study of Tibors' brother, Raimbaut d'Aurenga.[5] The last member of the group is an almost anonymous poet, La Compiuta Donzella. Her late thirteenth-century sonnets and a *tenzone* in sonnet form may be read in Contini's anthology.[6] We know very little about the dates, locations, and lives of these poets. The most complete presentation of available material is in Bogin's study.[7] Clues from which we may draw a picture exist in the *vidas* of Tibors, the Comtessa de Dia, Azalais de Porcairages, Lombarda, and Castelloza. A long *razo* treats the work of Maria de Ventadorn. Names of other *trobairitz* are given in the razos of Guiraut de Bornelh (Alamanda); Gui de Cavaillon (Garsenda); Elias de Barjols (also Garsenda) and Elias Cairel (Isabella).[8] One must, of course, treat the "factual data" occurring in the *vidas* and *razos* with caution.

Lyrics of the *trobairitz* as a group have been edited and published in Germany (1888), France (1946), and the United States (1976).[9] The three editions are somewhat at variance, for example, Jules Véran's French edition includes a *sirventès* in defense of Rome by Germonda of Montpellier which the American editor, Meg Bogin, excludes as "only of interest to church historians." A problem of interpretation exists with the lyric "Na Carenza al bel cors avinen." Véran names two speakers as authors while Bogin lists three. Both editions have special features: Véran includes lyrics by modern women poets writing in Provençal, while Bogin gives a long historical article and useful maps. The small corpus of twenty-four poems is divided almost evenly between *cansos* and *tensos*. We will take them up in that order.

The earliest song is a lovely fragment of a canso by Tibors that recalls, in tone and style, the famous sonnet "How do I love thee . . ." of Elizabeth Barrett Browning:

> Bels dous amics, ben vos posc en ver dir
> que anc non fo qu'ieu estes ses desir
> pos vos conven que us tenc per fin aman;
> ni anc no fo qu'ieu non agues talan,
> bels dous amics, qu'ieu soven no us vezes;
> ni anc no fo sazons que m'en pentis,
> ni anc no fo, se vos n'anes iratz,
> qu'ieu agues joi tro que fosetz tornatz;
> ni . . . [10]

Both lyrics create dramatic tension by caesural pauses and anaphora that reveals the obsession of desire:

> I love thee freely . . .
> I love thee purely . . .
> I love thee with the passion . . .

Tibors uses the negative, "que anc non fo . . . ni anc no fo . . .." The rhetorical strategy of both lyrics depends on strong and simple repetitions of openly expressed passion.

The enigmatic Comtessa de Dia has left four complete love songs. Exuberant word play and optimism pervade her lyrics. Grammatical rhymes:

> Ab joi et ab joven m'apais,
> e jois e jovens m'apaia,

and praise of herself and her lover:

> que mos amics es lo plus gais
> per qu'ieu sui coindet' e guaia,[11]

blend the syntactical adroitness of the Provençal male voice with the self-praise typical of the woman's voice in the anonymous dance songs. She chooses a lover who pleases her:

> Qu'ieu n'ai chausit un pro e gen,

but let him beware--she would leave him if he betrays her:

> qu'ieu fassa vas lui faillimen,
> sol non trob en lui faillensa.

She adopts the persona of a betrayed lover in the lyric "A chantar m'er do so qu'ieu non volria," a poem that has some of the motifs of Idyll II of Theocritus. The woman laments betrayal by her lover. Feeling tricked and cheated, she continues her self-defense and high self-praise, lauding her own steadfastness:

> . . . eu d'amar vos venssa
> lo mieus amics, car etz lo plus valens;

She knows her worth:

> Valer mi deu mos pretz e mos paratges,
> e ma beltatz e plus mos fis coratges,

and she wonders where to place the blame in him,

> non sai si s'es orguoills o mal talens.[12]

In another song, "Fin ioi me don' alegranssa," she turns the conventional figure of the gossip, the <u>lausengier</u>, to a source of amusement. Repudiating fear, she sings:

> e lor mals diz non m'esglaia:
> anz en son dos tanz plus gaia.

Gossipers are like a cloud that obscures the sun:

> com la niuols que s'espan
> qe·l solels en pert sa raia,

and she closes the poem with a threat of disaster to the other conventional enemy of love, the <u>gelos</u> (also <u>gilos</u> or <u>ialous</u>) the jealous man:

> E vos, gelos mal parlan, . . .
> per tal que dols vos deschaia.[13]

Christian Faucheux, in a study of the motifs and syntax of the lyrics of the Comtessa de Dia, finds the principal motifs to be "la souffrance, l'amour, la valeur du chevalier, l'infidelité, et la valeur de la dame.[14] Infidelity, separation, and persecution by the <u>lauzengiers</u> create the background for pain. However, all the lyrics close on a note of optimism, which can range from hope to joy. Her syntax shows a logical mind, both in choice of words and in causal propositions. She submits emotion to analysis. Even the few lyrics of this poet establish her as an important critic of <u>fin'amors</u> in the female voice.

The only other woman poet of whom we have more than one <u>canso</u> is Castelloza, who was from Le Puy in the Auvergne. She wrote after the Comtessa de Dia, and has a different tone, which Jeanroy disliked, calling it that of a "femme collante.[15] She continues the Provençal woman's self-praise, extolling her own faithfulness, her virtue, and high birth. Her tone is candid and she boldly speaks her mind:

> Amics, s'ie us troves avinen;
> humil e franc e de bona merce,
> be·us amera, quan era m'en.sove
> que·us trob vas mi mal e fellon e tric;

whether she is blaming the lover or praising him:

> Tot' autr' amor teing a nïen
> e sapchatz ben que mais jois no·m soste
> mas lo vostre que m'alegr' e·m reve.[16]

Each of her three songs makes reference to her songwriting. In the lyric "Amics, s'ie us trobes avinen," she writes to preserve the praises of the man who treats her badly:

> e fauc chanssos per tal qu'ieu fass' auzir
> vostre bon pretz, don ieu non posc sofrir
> que no·us fassa lauzar a tota gen.[17]

whereas in "Ja de chantar non degr' aver talan," she uses the paradox that the more she sings the worse she fares in love, but she continues to compose.[18] In "Mout avetz faich long estatge," she tells her former lover that he has made her famous because her suffering caused her to make songs.[19]

Castelloza's three songs may seem dull when viewed through Jeanroy's critical lens. A recent feminist critic reads her on the single plane of literalness, which is the same basis Jeanroy uses, and praises her willingness to take risks for love.[20] But if we read her three lyrics through the lens of the "carnival" function of the female voice, we find that her lyrics come to life. For instance, we hear a <u>double entendre</u> in her words in the lyric 'Mout avetz faich long estatge," as she compares herself unfavorably to other women lovers; she should know how to choose words better:

> Mout aurai mes mal usatge
> a las autras amairitz,
> qu'om sol trametre messatge
> emotz triatz e chausitz: [21]

Surely this is tongue-in-cheek humor from a poet who praises her own ability in every lyric of hers that has survived. Again, the self-posession and wit of the remark, later in the same poem, that since she writes good poetry out of her love suffering, her husband and family adore, ("fai grazir") the man. She closes the poem with an invitation to come back now that he has heard the song; "here, in the song" (and the audience understands by implication, <u>only</u> here in the song) he will find a good reception:

> e prec que venhatz a me,
> despois quez auretz auzida
> ma chanson, que·us fatz fionsa:
> sai trobetz bella semblansa. [21]

I believe there is much more subtle wit in her lyrics and a more playful use of convention than has been perceived by critics. A reading of this poem that assumes "straight" speech misses the humor of the carnavalesque female voice making fun of the male love song. Castelloza overturns convention again by asserting in two other lyrics the woman's right and pleasure in courting a man she has chosen:

> qu'el preiar ai un gran revenimen
> quan prec cellui don ai greu pessamen[22]

and

> que pois dompna s'ave
> d'amar, prejar deu be
> cavallier, s'en lui ve
> proez' e vassalatge. [23]

Far from a "femme collante," Castelloza projects a strong female persona who firmly holds the reins of her relationships by using the carnival values in the female voice.

The majority of the tensos are female/male dialogues in which, significantly, the woman speaks first. All concern the ethics and logistics of the love relation. The usual form is six stanzas of three sets of coblas doblas (two stanzas with matching rhymes) with a double tornada. Line length is between seven and eleven syllables with some patterns using a half-line in the third from last and the last lines. Rhymes are not the simple and traditional women's song binary pattern (aaab, abab, aaaaaab) of the female voice sung by the troubadour and trouvère. Rather, the Provençal woman poet composes her cansos and tensos in the rhyme patterns used by the Provençal male poet for male voice lyrics. The poems have crossed rhymes and couplets, such as abbaccddee, and abbaccdd. The one exception is a poem attributed to Alamanda, whose rhyme is aaaabab. It is a tenso with Guiraut de Bornelh, in which he speaks first.[24] The female speaker is a lady's maid who acts as intercessor between Guiraut and the absent domna. In accordance with what we have learned about low social status and the female voice, it would not be surprising if the rhyme pattern in this case were dictated by the thematics of the lyric.

One of the most interesting lyrics of this group is a tenso between Maria de Ventadorn and Gui d'Ussel, "Gui d'Ussel, be m pessa de vos," because we see the only example of the female speaker borrowing male speech. Maria uses a line of direct speech in a male persona, adopting a "single voiced" statement and giving it a new intention for her own purpose in her argument. The subject of the <u>tenso</u> is whether or not a lady has the right to court a man with whom she is in love. Maria poses the question in stanza one. Gui answers with a strong affirmative that calls for reciprocity in love, "qu'en dos amics non deu aver maior." She agrees in the next stanza, with the statement "e dompna deu a son drut far honor / cum ad amic, mas non cum a seignor." Then Gui begins the topic of unequal love relations in reply to wnich Maria humorously describes a new lover on his knees before his lady:

> mans jointas e de genolhos:
> "Dompna, voillatz que·us serva francamen com
> lo vostr' om," el ell' enaissi·l pren;[25]

She has taken a line of "ready-made" speech familiar to her audience, imbued it with her own intention so that it will serve her polemic in its new context. The opportunities for comic effects in gesture and intonation are unmistakable. She gives us a rare view of the world from the eye of a wise and witty medieval woman. Maria closes the poem by saying that reciprocity in love cannot be combined with a "begging servant" attitude. This <u>tenso</u> is surely one of the most charming presentations of the love ethic of reciprocity, a theme that plays a larger place in medieval courtly lyric than has been recognized.

A beautiful duet between a lady and her lover is the <u>tenso</u> "Vos que.m semblatz dels corals amadors" by Garsenda, b. ca. 1170.[26] She wishes he were not so timid:

> Vos que.m semblatz dels corals amadors,
> ja non volgra que fossetz tan doptanz;

and she argues that he will lose her if he does not speak up, for a lady is afraid to speak for what she wants:

> que ges dompna non ausa descobrir
> tot so qu'il vol per paor de faillir.

His reply is tender and bashful; she is high born:

> Bona dompna, vostr' onrada valors
> mi fai temeros estar, tan es granz,

and he only wishes deeds rather than words could do the courting, "qu'us honratz faitz deu be valer un dir." Garsenda was the wife of Alphonse II of Provence, brother of King Pedro II of Aragon. After her husband's death in 1209, she was the ruler of Provence, a formidable <u>dompna</u>!

Isabella and Elias Cairel engage in a mutual mudslinging *tenso* "N'Elias Cairel, de l'amor."[27] They pose as former lovers, now trading invective. Rapid dialogue of the "He said/she said" domestic comedy is a time-honored source of fun. In stanza one "she says" that he does not sound so good anymore, "que vostre chanz non vai si com solia," and to this challenge he replies that he only sang praise of her to gain honor and advantage:

> en mon chantar, no·l dis per drudaria
> mas per honor e pro qu'ieu n'atendia,

to which she says he is mad, "mas ben podetz doblar vostra follia," and he replies that it would be mad to stay in her clutches, and he is going to see a pretty lady. She tells him to go back to his monastery, "bon conseil vos daria / que tornassetz estar en la badia," to which he says that she will soon need one, "qu'en breu temps perdretz la color." The standard jokes of musical comedy are apparently timeless.[28] She asks for the name of his new lover so she can decide on her qualities, but he gives his good reasons for not telling.

The *sirventès* "Greu m'es a durar" of Gormonda of Montpellier is interesting for a number of reasons, which Véran explains in his edition.[29] An example of a political poem written by a woman, it serves to dispel the conventional view that poetry by women is confined to "domestic" themes. As a response to Guillem Figueira's "D'un sirventes far en est son que m'agenssa," it presents a pro-Roman Catholic view of the crusade against the heterodox Cathars. Gormonda's city, Montpellier, like the city of Nïmes, was never involved in Catharism. It was an independent city under the protection of the bishops of Maguelone, and supported neither the northern French army nor the forces of Toulouse. Writing between the dates of September 1227 and January 1229, according to Jules Véran, Gormonda modeled her poem on the virulent work of Figueira. She wrote twenty stanzas (twenty-three in Figueira), and places the word *Roma* at the beginning of thirteen stanzas (it comes first in twenty-one of his stanzas). The form of her stanza is:

> a b   a b   a b   c c c b   c
> 5 6' 5 6' 5 6' 5 5 5 6' 5

The stanzas are linked by rhyme; the first verse of a stanza takes the rhyme of the last verse of the preceding stanza—in this technique of *coblas capcaudadas*. The first two stanzas follow:

> Greu m'es a durar,
> quan aug tal descrezensa
> dir ni semenar.
> e no'm platz ni m'agensa

> qu'om non deu amar
> qui fai desmantenensa
> a so don totz bes
> ven e nais e es
> salvamens e fes.
> Per qu'ieu farai parvensa
> e semblan que'm pes.
>
> No us meravilhes
> negus si eu muou guerra
> ab fals mal apres
> qu'a son poder soterra
> totz bos faitz cortes
> els encauss' e'ls enserra;
> trop se fenh arditz
> quar de Roma ditz
> mal, qu'es caps e guitz
> de totz selhs que en terra
> an bos esperitz.

Gormonda's poem is a case of extreme inter-textuality. As well as being by far the longest poem of the *trobairitz* corpus, the *sirventès* documents the *trobairitz*'s participation in public discussion of the momentous events of the Albigensian war.

This brief examination of some of the *cansos* and *tensos* written by Provençal women poets indicates the extreme interest of the corpus. While the size of the sample may prevent us from regarding it as truly representative, a few generalizations are possible. The lyrics are written in styles marked by individuality within the limits of contemporary culture. The *trobairitz* wrote no extant *pastorelas* or *malmariée* songs, genres used by dozens of male troubadours. In the poems we have, they use no archaic speech, foreign language, or dialectal variant, three speech styles frequent in the female speech *persona* in lyrics by troubadours. On the contrary, their linguistic style is correct, standard Provençal poetic usage. The exclamatory, breathlessly spontaneous, and urgent tone often rising to incantation and rhetorical appeal to nature has no place in their poetic speech. Let us consider some recent critical views of the *trobairitz* to find a ground for discussion of questions of interpretation.

Marianne Shapiro writes of the *cansos* of the *trobairitz* that their "unconventionality proceeds from omission.[30] In answer to the Jeanroy/Ferrante thesis that the women poets reversed the terms of courtly love, raising their lovers to paradigmatic status, Shapiro concludes that they do not simply reverse roles. The problem their *cansos* had to solve was how to plead a woman's love in the face of two male-determined cultural evaluations: 1) the non-amorous lady of the troubadour *canso* (this is Shapiro's view with which I do not agree), and 2) the excessively erotic female of Church dogmatics, being both object of pursuit and lover. To overcome this contradiction, the trobairitz choose an intermediate state, neither cold nor excessively erotic, as a ground of strife on which to defend their feelings. Their speech, even in cansos, is aggressive and their stance agonistic. They defend by negation, using a style that includes commonplace, polemic, and a lack of dense figural force. She notes the omissions: only one nature opening, no address to a public, two dedications to female patrons, and none to male patrons, only one senhal, Castelloza's Bel Noms. She assesses the contribution of the trobairitz negatively, suggesting that they were unable to establish a conventional voice for women poets, and were forgotten by the time of the Renaissance poets Louise Labé, Victoria Colonna, and Gaspara Stampa. (We should note, however, that almost all twelfth and thirteenth-century literature fell under the same neglect.)

In her article on the trobairitz, Kittye delle Robbins broaches the question of why these few poems and poets survive in the overwhelmingly male-dominated courtly lyric.[31] The problem can be seen in two lights: either the group of twenty is small compared to the hundreds of named male troubadours, or it is large, given the dearth of women poets in the long history of recorded poetry; centuries when women had almost no access to writing. Indeed, literacy is a factor that Marianne Shapiro believes contributed to the rise of women poets in Occitania. Noting the absence of direct address and audience-related terms found in poets such as Guilhelm IX, Shapiro suggests that the trobairitz wrote for a reading public but did not perform in public. Charles Camproux argues that the "astonishing audacity" of the trobairitz can be traced to the metaphysical "promotion féminine" of the courtly love ethic which lifted women to a symbolic equality with men in a utopian "civilisation du Joi d'Amor.[32] Robbins qualifies this argument with the point that while we must not confuse symbolic with actual power, the trobairitz were indeed beginning to exercise a "prise de la parole" in reaching for verbal autonomy. She then carries the Camproux focus on the putative role of women further with the interesting suggestion that the very presence of the domna as a silent target of male aspiration provoked a verbal response. Implicit within the male monologue would be the dialogical situation. an answering voice which the trobairitz supplied. The "grand chant courtois" would depend, in this view, on a tacit reciprocity uniting the lover and the lady, poet and audience, singer and song. The very absence of the lady's speech anticipates and calls for her refutation. Robbins writes, ". . . the male poet bestowed on the lady . . . a powerful hallucinatory presence within the lyric paradigm." The figure of the lady is potentially a subject within the lyric style that most reifies her.

All these arguments suffer from one large objection. They give reasons for the existence of trobairitz in conditions which prevailed in courts throughout Romance-speaking countries: but the women poets appeared in Occitania only. The disproportion of women poets in the Romance literatures can be seen in the following table:

Table 4

LYRICS BY WOMEN POETS IN MEDIEVAL ROMANCE LITERATURES

LANGUAGE	NUMBER OF POETS	NUMBER OF SONGS
1. Mozarabic-Spanish	0	0
2. Provençal	19	24
3. Old French	3	4
4. Galician-Portuguese	0	0
5. Italian	2	4

While we could not reasonably expect any poetry by women in the Mozarabic-Spanish corpus, we should be impressed by the absence of women poets in Galician-Portuguese, and the almost total absence of women poets in Old French, Sicilian, and Italian lyric, in view of the remarkable number, for a pre-modern society, in Provençal.

The factors that have been advanced for the existence of a group of women poets in Occitania, namely literacy (Shapiro), "promotion féminine" (Camproux), and "recurrent evocation" (Robbins), may well have contributed to an environment in which women could become poets. They are powerful material and psychological elements. But if we look at the development of courtly lyric in the Romance literatures as a whole, we must explain why the same factors had dissimilar results in other areas. The influence of the model of female speech has not been considered, and it is a significant, if not determining, factor. The contours of this model vary from one Romance language to another. Like anything living, the female voice is plastic, shaped according to the felt needs in any particular culture. The song style for female speech in Provençal differs from that in Old French and Galician-Portuguese, and I would suggest that the difference permitted literate women gifted as songwriters to exercise their talent. They could find an emotional and stylistic ground on which to build a poetic expression. I have mentioned this topic in the pages devoted to the female voice in Provençal in Chapter Three, "Persona--Part One," and will here cite three areas of comparison: first, a rationalizing versus incantatory axis of intonation, second, the dramatic role of the pastora, and third, the presence or absence of large numbers of conventional songs in the female voice.[33]

The tonal quality of the woman's lament in Provençal is less desperate and more self-conscious than its counterpart in other literatures. Within the beautiful and haunting lyrics, we find the woman seeking reasons and explanations for the loss of love. Her voice is self-aware; she wants to know the causes of her experience. A comparison of two analogous laments, one from Provençal lyric and one from Galician-Portuguese, will illustrate the "rationalizing" element in the female voice in Provençal. Both songs are sung by an abandoned woman on a beach who appeals to the waves for news of her lover. In the Galician-Portuguese lyric, Martin Codax' "Ondas do mar de Vigo," a three-part pattern is used in each of the four stanzas: 1) an address to the waves, 2) interrogation of the waves, and 3) exclamation of sorrow. For example, stanza one:

    Ondas do mar de Vigo   (address)
    Se vistes meu amigo?   (interrogation)
    E ai Deus, se verra cedo![34]   (exclamation)

This pattern, repeated in each of four stanzas, creates a powerful, emotional tone. The Provençal song, "Altas ondas que venez sus la mar," generally attributed to Raimbaut de Vaqueiras, has a different address in each of the three stanzas, 1) to the waves, 2) to the wind, and 3) to the world at large and the woman's conscience.[35] The change in the third stanza brings about an abrupt variation in tone. Beginning with an abstract statement, the speaker says that a foreigner makes a bad lover because his joy will turn to tears. She then illustrates this general principle with her own experience, saying that she gave him her love, never thinking that he would leave her. The Latinate syntax of "car . . ." and "e . . .e" and the verb "cudey" in a past tense introduce a reasoning tone. Objective analysis of her unhappy experience with the use of general truths is, I believe, a distinguishing characteristic of the lament in Provençal literature.

Again in the anonymous lament "Quan vei los praz verdesir," we find analytic statement followed by a reflection on personal experience. After a "call to the lover" and a description of her sufferings, the female speaker states two general rules: 1) a woman in love needs a strong heart, and 2) a woman not in love should guard herself from falling in love:

    1)   Domna que amors aten
           ben deu aver fin coratge

    2)   Domna qui amic non a
           ben si gart que mais non aja.[36]

These abstractions are all the more remarkable because they are set in a song of archaic features: parallelistic diction and a refrain "Aei!" which establish a highly emotional tone. Indeed, the tendency to parallelism is visible in the theoretical verses, both beginning "Domna / ben . . .Domna / ben."

Anna Granville Hatcher, in her article, "Marcabru's 'A la fontana del vergier," describes this crusade lament as a woman's song.[37] She points out that the woman blames successively Jesus (line 17), St. Louis (line 26) and God (line 37) for her lover's absence. No promises of earthly or heavenly delights distract her mind, and she stays firmly within her particular situation. In the last line of the song, she carries the sequence of blame to its limit; the man who left her must not have regarded her very highly:

> . . .mas pauc mi tey
> Que trop s'es de mi alonhatz.

In her feeling of self-worth, her independent judgments and her analysis of concrete particulars in her situation, she represents a typical voice of Provençal women poets.

If we put beside the lamenting woman in Marcabru's poem the song "A chantar m'er do so" of the Comtessa de Dia, we have a striking example of the same high self-esteem and freedom of mind. She neither excuses nor castigates her lover or condemns "men in general," but she wants to know the cause of their separation:

> Valer me deu mos pretz e mos paratges
> E ma beltetz, e plus mos fis coratges
>
> Ieu vuoill saber, lo mieus bels amics gens
> Perque vos m'etz tant fers ni tant salvatges.[38]

She does not deny her affections, or claim that suffering will ennoble her mind; she pursues her need to understand her situation in specific detail.

The speaker of Clara D'Anduze's lyric "En greu esmai et en greu pessamen" laments her lover's absence and protests her marital helplessness. She would hide her body from her husband if she could, "tals l'a que jamais non l'auria." In a display of lucid analysis, she describes the effect of her anger on her creative power:

> Amicstan ai d'ira e de feunia
> quar no vos vey, que quan; ieu cug chantar,
> planh e sospir; perqu'ieu no puesc so far
> ab mas coblas que,l cors complir volria.[39]

She is not able to complete an entire song, but can only achieve stanzas "no puesc so far / ab mas coblas," because of the interference of her power-destroying anger. The subtle play of the phrase "que 1 cors complir volris" is humorous; it can be understood that she would like with her heart to finish the song, but also that her body would like to complete the song's meaning, i.e., to express love.

The countrywoman of the Old French _pastourelle_ has quite a different character from the female speaker of the Provençal _pastorela_, a fact on which a number of critics have commented. The Provençal _toza_, in the earliest examples of the medieval Romance lyric, is the sharp-tongued _vilana_ of Marcabru's "L'autrier jost' una sebissa." She carries the "otherness" of reported speech in her economic class _(vilana)_ physical description _(mestissa)_, and social heterodoxy. But in verbal assertiveness and strength of self-defence, she is more than the equal of her debate partner. In Bakhtin's terms, "contamination" from the general qualities of male speech in Provençal--colorful, even aggressive speech-has passed into the female speech voice. As late as the close of the thirteenth century, one hundred and fifty years after the Marcabru lyric, the Provençal _tozas_ heard in Giraut Riquier's series of six _pastorelas_ follow the indigenous style of Provençal female speech.[40] The genre in Galician-Portuguese and Old French, however, shows the loss of verbal strength and the substitution of a weeping, irritated, or victimized _pastora_ who more often than not loses the verbal contest with her interlocutor. The narrator of el rei Don Dinis' "Ua pastor se queixava" introduces the _pastora_ thus:

> Ela s' estava queixando,
> come molher con gram coita
> e que a pesar, des quando
> nacera, non fora doita,
> por en dezia chorando!
> "Tu non es se non mia coita,
>   ai, amor!"[41]

While the poet of the _pastorela_ in Provençal maintains interest at the textual level of verbal forensics, in an attitude of sunny good humor, the French poet lets the story take over. Variants in the scenario are numerous; additional characters, rustic games, musical instruments, etc. The female speaker is no longer the inventive, lively talker who confounds the eager suitor with the resources of her wit. After singing her incantatory and "pivotal" snatch of song, the French _bergère_ may call for help, submit with protest, or with pleasure, to the advances of the suitor, but she is no longer equal to the task of verbal supremacy.

Not only does the model of female speech change its character in conventional songs, but the quantitative change is so remarkable that it should be noticed.⁴² In Provençal, a number of vivid examples of songs with female speech are known, but in Galician-Portuguese and Old French we find literally hundreds of <u>partidas</u> (songs of leaving and arrival), songs of a <u>malmariée</u> and the <u>pastourelles</u>. The immense popularity of these songs coincided, it seems, with the rise of centripetal forces creating courtly power centers, forces which actively took power from the smaller local communities. The continuous replaying of the drama of the local girl who has lost her lover to the power of the king explained the new state of affairs. The Old French <u>pastourelle</u> likewise reinforced the relations between newly powerful men and newly inferior women. The great paradox here is that the female voice, which represents <u>carnival</u> and its values, also, by virtue of being a minority voice, upholds the repressive action of hierarchical stratification. It exists as rebellion held in check. or willing or doleful submission to a stronger, space-occupying male voice.

The speech atmosphere created by the female voice in the different Romance literatures. then, differs in its liberating or repressive effect on potential women poets according to the kind of "contamination" it undergoes. What about Italian lyric? Here we find the lamenting female speech, caused by physical absence of the lover or by a forced marriage to an unwanted husband. In the vulgar songs. a raucous or begging tone creates a negative speech image for potential women poets.

The abstractions of <u>dolce stil novo</u>, which focusses attention on, and hence valorizes, the inner state of the male lover, reduces the role of the silent, ideal <u>donna</u> to a catalyst of the movements in the lover's heart. The all-important theme is the effect of love on the cognitive processes of the self-absorbed male. It is indicative of the impotence of <u>dolce stil novo</u> to inspire dialogue with female speech that Dante goes back to the early Provençal model of vigorous and fearless speech for Beatrice in her encounter with Dante in <u>Purgatorio</u>.

It is probable that the model of female speech that valorizes assertiveness and rationality gave the incentive to participation in public song to women of wealth and rank in Occitania. Women in other areas, with the same gifts, contronted with a speech model characterized by anxiety, lament, submission, and archaic or primitive styles were negatively conditioned for song composition. We are only on the threshold of understanding the process by which cultures encourage or discourage women's participation in public speech. Much work remains to be done as evidence accumulates. Different legal and social customs--such as the ability of women to inherit property in Southern France--may well have contributed to the existence of <u>trobairitz</u> in Provençal literature and to their absence from other

Romance-speaking areas. The present study is only a part of a larger theoretical investigation.

Notes to Chapter 5

1   Three historical anthologies of poetry by women are the result of recent research: A Book of Women Poets from Antiquity to Now, Aliki and Willis Barnstone, eds. (New York: Schocken, 1980); The Penguin Book of Women Poets, eds. Carol Cosman, with Joan Keefe, Kathleen Weaver, Joanna Bankier, Doris Earnshaw, and Deirdre Lashgari; Women Poets of the World, eds. Joanna Bankier and Deirdre Lashgari, with Doris Earnshaw, (New York: Macmillan, 1983).

2   See Kenneth Jackson, The Gododdin, p. 46-7.

3   The most complete collection of contemporary women poets is The Other Voice: Twentieth-Century Women Poets in Translation, eds. Joanna Bankier, Carol Cosman, Doris Earnshaw, Joan Keefe, Deirdre Lashgari, and Kathleen Weaver (New York: W. W. Norton, 1976).

4   See Mikhail Bakhtin, Problems of Dostoevsky's Poetics, trans. R. W. Rotsel (Ann Arbor, Mich.: Ardis, 1973) esp. Chapter 2, "The Hero and the Author's Position in Relation to the Hero."

5   Walter Pattison, The Life and Works of the Troubadour Raimbaut d'Orange (Minneapolis: 1952).

6   Gianfranco Contini, Poeti del Duecento, vol. 1, pp. 434-5.

7   Meg Bogin, The Women Troubadours, pp. 160-169.

8   Jean Boutière and A. H. Schutz, Biographies des troubadours, textes provençaux des XIIIe et XIVe siècles, (Toulouse, 1950).

9   The three editions are: Oscar Schultz-Gora, Die Provenzalischen Dichterinnen (Leipzig, 1888); Jules Véran, Les Poétesses Provençales du moyen âge et de nos jours (Paris, 1946); Meg Bogin, The Women Troubadours (New York: Paddington Press, 1976).

10 Bogin, p. 80.

11 Bogin, pp. 82-4.

12 Bogin, pp. 84-7.

13 Bogin, pp. 90-91.

14 Christian Fauchaux, "Etude sémantique et syntaxique de l'oeuvre de la Comtesse de Die," Signum 1 (1974) No. 1, 1-17, and No. 2, 5-16.

15   Alfred Jeanroy, Histoire Sommaire de la Poésie Occitane (Paris: Didier, 1945) p. 78.

16   Bogin, pp. 118-21.

17   Bogin, p. 118.

18   Bogin, p. 122.

19   Bogin, p. 126.

20   Bogin, p. 72. "Castelloza is almost modern in her pursuit of a passionate attachment in which the self is risked."

21   Bogin, p. 128.

22   Bogin, p. 118.

23   Bogin, p. 124.

24   Bogin, p. 102.

25   Bogin, p. 100.

26   Bogin, p. 108.

27   Bogin, p. 110.

28   Two examples of contemporary male/female comic songs are "Run That by Me One More Time," an early Dolly Parton song, and "Anything You Can Do, I Can Do Better," from the musical "Annie, Get Your Gun."

29   Jules Véran, Les Poétesses Provençales, pp. 196-201. The following historical information is taken from Véran's introduction to the poem.

30   Marianne Shapiro, "The Provençal Trobairitz and the Limits of Courtly Love," Signs (Spring, 1978) pp. 560-571.

31   Kittye delle Robbins "Love's Martyrdoms Revised: Conversion, Inversion, and Subversion of Trobador style in Trobairitz Poetry," unpublished article, pp. 9-11.

32   Charles Camproux, Le Joi d'amor des troubadours, (Montpellier: Causse et Castelnau, 1965) pp. 95-103, quoted by delle Robbins.

33   See Chapter Three, of this work.

34   Nunes, Cantigas d'amigo, 491

35 Hill and Bergin, <u>Anthology of the Provençal Troubadours</u>, I, p. 164.

36 Bartsch, <u>Chresthomatie</u>, p. 227.

37 Anna Granville Hatcher, "Marcabru's 'A la fontana del vergier'" <u>Modern Language Notes</u> 79 (1964), 284-95.

38 Bogin, p. 86.

39 Bogin, p. 130.

40 Martín de Riquer, <u>Los Trovadores</u>, vol. 3, pp. 1624-1646.

41 Nunes, <u>Cantigas d'amigo</u>, 1.

42 Pierre Bec notes the small number of <u>chansons de femme</u> in Provençal lyric (<u>La Lyrique française au moyen âge</u>, vol. 1, p. 53). Bec suggests that the cause is accidental only, due to the loss of manuscripts.

BIBLIOGRAPHY

Primary Sources

Appel, Carl. *Provenzalische Chrestomathie mit Abriss der Formenlehre und Glossar.* 6th ed. Leipzig, 1932.

Audiau, Jean. *Nouvelle anthologie des troubadours.* Paris: Delagrave, 1928.

Bartsch, Karl. *Chrestomathie de l'ancien français, VIIIe-XVe siècle.* Leipzig, 1886.

_____. *Altfranzösische Romanzen und Pastourellen.* (Leipzig: Vogel, 1870); rpt. Geneva: Slatkine Reprints, 1973.

Bec, Pierre. *La Lyrique française au moyen âge (XIIe-XIIIe siècles: Contribution a une typologie des genres poétiques médiévaux.* 2 vols. Paris: Picard, 1977.

Bogin, Meg. *The Women Troubadours.* New York: Paddington Press, 1976.

Contini, Gianfranco. *Poeti del Duecento.* 2 vols. Milan: Ricciardi, 1960.

Hill, Raymond T. and Thomas G. Bergin. *Anthology of the Provençal Troubadours.* Yale Romanic Studies, 2nd ser. No. 23. 2nd ed. Ed. Thomas G. Bergin, et al. 2 vols. New Haven and London: Yale Univ. Press, 1973.

Monaci, Ernesto. *Crestomazia italiana dei primi secoli.* Rome: Societa Ed. Dante Alighieri, 1955.

Monroe, James T. "Two New Bilingual Harǧas (Arabic and Romance) in Arabic Muwaṡṡaha." *Hispanic Review,* 42 (1974), 243-264.

René Nelli and René Lavaud. *Les Troubadours. II: Le Trésor poétique de l'Occitanie.* n.p.: Desclée De Brouwer, 1966.

Nunes, José Joaquim. *Cantigas d'amigo dos trovadores galego-portugueses.* 2 vols. Coimbra: Imprensa da Universidade, 1926.

Panvini, Bruno. *Le rime della scuola siciliana.* 2 vols. Florence: Olschki, 1962 and 1964.

Riquer, Martín de. *Los Trovadores: Historia literaria y textos.* 3 vols. Barcelona: Planeta, 1975.

Sola Solé, José María. *Corpus de poésia mozárabe: les ḫarǰa-s andalusíes.* Barcelona: Ediciones Hispam, 1973.

Spanke, Hans. Eine altfranzösische Liedersammlung der anonyme teil K N P X. Halle: Niemeyer, 1925.

Véran, Jules. Les Poétesses Provençales du moyen âge et de nos jours. Paris: Librarie Aristide Quillet, 1946.

Zink, Michel. Belle: essai sur les chansons de toile, suivi d'une édition et d'une traduction. Paris: Champion, 1978.

Secondary Sources

Adorno, Theodor. Einleitung in die Musiksoziologie. Frankfurt: Suhrkamp, 1962. Trans. E. B. Ashton, Introduction to the Sociology of Music. New York: The Seabury Press, 1976.

Agonito, Rosemary. History of Ideas on Women: A Source Book. New York: Putnam, 1977.

Ashley, Kathleen. "The Role of the Courts and the 13th Century Portuguese Lyric." ACTA, 3 (1976), 65-78.

Bagley, Cynthia P. "Cantigas de Amigo and Cantigas de Amor." Bulletin of Hispanic Studies, 43 (1966) 241-252.

Bec, Pierre. "Le Type lyrique des chansons de femme dans la poésie du moyen âge." Mélanges...Labande. Poitiers: 1974 (13-23).

_____. "Genres et registres dans la lyrique médiévale des XIIe et XIIIe siècles: essai de classement typologique." Revue de linguistique romane, 38 (1974), 26-39.

Biella, Ada. "Considerazioni sull'origine e sulla diffusione della pastorella." Cultura Neolatina, 25 (1965), 236-267.

Bloch, Howard. Medieval French Literature and the Law. Berkeley: University of California Press, 1977.

Boase, Roger. Origin and Meaning of Courtly Love. Manchester: Manchester Univ. Press, 1977.

Boklund, Karin. "Socio-sémiotique du roman courtois." Sémiotica, 21 (1977), 227-256.

_____. "On the Spatial and Cultural Characteristics of Courtly Romance." Sémiotica, 20 (1977), 1-38.

Boutière, Jean, and Alexander H. Schutz. Biographies des troubadours, textes provençaux des XIIIe et XIVe siècles. 2nd ed. Les Classiques d'Oc, 1. Paris: 1964; 1st ed. Bibliothèque Méridionale, 27. Toulouse, 1950.

Bowra, Cecil M. *The Medieval Love Song*. London: Athlone, 1961.

_____. *Primitive Song*. Cleveland and New York: World, 1962.

Briffault, Robert. *Les troubadours et le sentiment romanesque*. Paris: 1945.

Buffum, D. L. *Le Roman de la Violette ou de Gérard de Nevers by Gerbert de Montreuil*. Paris: SATF, 1928.

Cantarino, Vicente. "The Composition of Andalusian Muwashshahas with a Romance Kharja." *Kentucky Romance Quarterly*, 21 (1974), 447-68.

Cardoso, Wilton. *Da Cantiga de Seguir no cancioneiro peninsular da idade media*. n.p.: Belo Horizonte, 1977.

Chailley, Jacques. *Histoire musicale du moyen âge*. 2nd ed. Paris: PUF, 1969.

Chambers, Frank. "Imitation of Form in the Old Provençal Lyric." *Romance Philology* 6, 2 and 3. (1952-3), 104-20.

Chaytor, Henry John. *From Script to Print*. Cambridge: Cambridge University Press, 1945.

Clarke, Dorothy Clotelle. "Versification of the Hargas in the Monroe-Swiatlo Collection of Arabic Hargas in Hebrew Muwassahs Compared with that of Early Hispano-Romance Poetry." *Journal of the American Oriental Society*, 98 (1978), 35-49.

Cluzel, Irenée-Marcel and Leon Pressouyre. *La Poésie lyrique d'oil, les origines et les premiers trouvères, textes d'étude*. Paris: 1962.

Coirault, Patrice. "Belle Aelis et sa posterité folklorique." *Romance Philology*, 2 (1949), 299-304.

"The Comic Spirit in Medieval France." *L'Esprit Créateur*, 16 (1976).

Compton, Linda Fish. *Andalusian Lyrical Poetry and Old Spanish Love Songs: The Muwashshah and its Kharja*. New York: New York University Press, 1976.

Cremonesi, Carla. "Chansons de geste e chansons de toile." *Studi Romanzi*, 30 (1943), 55-203.

Cullman, Arthur. *Die Lieder und Romanzen des Audefroi le Bastard*. Halle: Niemeyer, 1914.

Cummins, John. The Spanish Traditional Lyric. Oxford: Pergamon, 1977.

Dähne, Rudolf. Die Lieder der Maumariée seit dem mittelalter. Halle: Niemeyer, 1933.

[Davenson, Henri. Les Troubadours. Paris: Editions du Seuil, 1961. (see Marrou, Henri.)]

Delbouille, Maurice. "A propos des origines de la lyrique romane: tradition 'populaire' ou tradition 'cléricale.'" Marche Romane, 20 (1970), 13-27.

Denomy, Alexander. "Concerning the Accessibility of Arabic Influences to the Earliest Provençal Troubadours." Mediaeval Studies, 15 (1953), 147-158.

Deyermond, Alan. "The Earliest Lyric and its Descendants." In A Literary History of Spain, vol. I, The Middle Ages. London: Benn; New York: Barnes and Noble, 1971, pp. 1-30.

_____. "Pero Meogo's Stags and Fountains: Symbol and Anecdote in the Traditional Lyric." Romance Philology 33 (1979). 265-283.

D'Heur, Jean-Marie. Troubadours d'oc et troubadours galiciens-portugais: Recherches sur quelques échanges dans la littérature de l'Europe au moyen âge. Cultura medieval e moderna, 1. Paris: 1973.

_____. Nomenclature des troubadours galiciens-portugais (XIIe-XIVe siècles). Table de concordance de leurs chansonniers, et liste des incipit de leurs compositions. Arquivos do Centro Cultural Portugues, 7. Paris, 1973, p. 17-100.

Dragonetti, Roger. La Technique poétique des trouvères dans la chanson courtoise. Bruges, 1960.

Dronke, Peter. Medieval Latin and the Rise of European Love-Lyric. 2 vols. Oxford: Clarendon, 1965.

Duby, Georges. Medieval Marriage: Two Models from Twelfth-Century France. Trans. Elborg Forster. Baltimore: Johns Hopkins Univ. Press, 1978.

Duckworth, George. The Nature of Roman Comedy. Princeton: Princeton University Press, 1952.

Dutton, Brian. "Some New Evidence for the Romance Origins of the Muwashshahas." BHS, 42 (1965), 73-81.

Erickson, Carolly. The Medieval Vision: Essays in History and Perception. New York: Oxford University Press, 1976.

Family and Society: Selections from the Annales Economies, Sociétés, Civilisations. Trans. Elborg Forster and Patricia M. Ranum. Ed. Robert Forster and Orest Ranum. Baltimore: Johns Hopkins University Press, 1976.

Faral, Edmond. "Les Chansons de toile ou chansons d'histoire." Romania, 69 (1946-7), 433-62.

Fauchaux, Christian. "Etude sémantique et syntaxique de l'oeuvre de la Comtesse de Die." Signum (Royal Military College, Kingston, Canada). 1 (1974), No. 1, 1-17, and No. 2, 5-16.

La Femme dans les civilisations des Xe-XIIIe siècles. Actes du colloque tenu à Poitiers, 23-25 sept. 1976. Publications du Centre d'Etudes Supérieures de Civilisation Médiévale, 8. Poitiers: Université de Poitiers, 1977.

Françon, Marcel. "Sur la structure du rondeau." Romance Notes, 10 (1968), 147.

Frank, Istvan. Répertoire métrique de la poésie des troubadours. 2 vols. Bibliothèque de l'Ecole des Hautes Etudes, 302 and 308. Paris, 1953 and 1957.

Frappier, Jean. La poésie lyrique en France aux XIIe et XIIIe siècles. Paris: C D U, 1963.

Frenk Alatorre, Margit. Lírica hispánica de tipo popular: Edad Media y Renacimiento. Mexico City: Univ. Nacional Autonoma, 1966.

_____. "La autenticidad folklórica de la antigua lírica 'popular.'" Annuario de Letras, 6 (1968-9), 148-69.

_____. Las jarchas mozárabes y los comienzos de la lírica románica. Mexico City: El Colegio de México, 1975.

_____. "Jaryas Mozárabes y Estribillos Franceses." Nueva Revista de Filología Hispánico, 6 (1952), 281-4.

Frings, Theodor. Minnesinger und Troubadours. Deutsche Academie der Wissenschaften, Vorträge und Schriften, 34. Berlin, 1949.

Gangutia Elícegui, Elvira. "Poesía griega 'de amigo' y poesía arábigo-española." Emérita. 40 (1972), 329-96.

García Gómez, Emilio. Las jarchas romances de la serie árabe en su marco. Madrid: Sociedad de Estudios y Publicaciones, 1965. 2nd ed. Barcelona: Seix Barral, 1975.

Gerold, Théodore. La Musique au moyen âge. Paris: Champion, 1932.

Giffen, Lois Anita. Theory of Profane Love Among the Arabs. New York University Studies in Near Eastern Civilization, No. 3. New York: New York University Press, 1976.

Gillespie, Gerald. "Origins of Romance Lyrics: A Review of Research." Yearbook of Comparative and General Literature, 16 (1967), 16-32.

Goldin, Frederick. Lyrics of the Troubadours and Trouvères: An Anthology and a History. New York: Anchor Press, 1973.

Guiette, Robert. D'une poésie formelle en France au moyen âge. Paris, 1972. First printed in Revue des sciences humaines 54 (1949) 61-9; repr. with add. text in Romanica gandensia 8 (1960) 9-32.

Hanning, Robert. The Individual in 12th Century Romance. New Haven and London: Yale University Press, 1977.

Hatto, Arthur T., ed. Eos: An Enquiry into the Theme of Lovers' Meetings and Partings at Dawn in Poetry. The Hague, 1965.

Heger, Klaus. "Die bisher veröffentlichten Hargas und ihre Deutungen." ZRPh. Beihefte 101. Tübingen, 1960.

Jackson, William T. H. "The Medieval Pastourelle as a Satirical Genre." Philological Quarterly, 51 (1952).

Jahiel, Edwin. "French and Provençal Pcet-Musicians of the Middle Ages: A Biblio-Discography." Romance Philology, 14 (1961), 200-07.

Jeanroy, Alfred. Les Origines de la poésie lyrique en France au moyen âge. Etudes de littérature française et comparée. 3rd. ed. Paris, 1925.

Joly, Raymond. "Les chansons d'histoire." Romanistisches Jährbuch, 12 (1961), pp. 51-66.

Jonin, Pierre. "Le refrain dans les chansons de toile." Romania, 96 (1975), 209-441.

Key, Mary Ritchie. Male/Female Language. New Jersey: Scarecrow Press, 1975.

Köhler, Erich. "Observations historiques et sociologiques sur la poésie des troubadours." Cahiers de civilisation médiévale, 7 (1964), 27-51.

Lakoff, Robin. Language and Woman's Place. New York: Harper and Row, 1975.

_____. "Language and Sexual Identity." Semiotica, 19 (1977).

Langbaum, Robert. The Poetry of Experience. New York: Norton, 1957.

Lazar, Moshé. Amour courtois et 'fin'amors' dans la littérature du XIIe siècle. Bibliothèque Français et Romane, Ser. C. Etudes littéraire, 8. Paris: Klincksieck, 1964.

Lecoy, Felix. Jean Renart: Le Roman de la Rose ou de Guillaume de Dole. Paris: Champion, 1962.

Le Gentil, Pierre. La Poésie lyrique espagnole et portugaise a la fin du moyen âge. 2 vols. Rennes: Plihon, 1953.

_____. Le virelai et le villancico: Le problème des origines arabes. Paris: Belles Lettres, 1954.

_____. "La strophe zadjalesque et les khardjas." Romania, 84 (1963), 1-27, 209-50, 409-11.

Linker, Robert White. A Bibliography of Old French Lyrics. Romance Monographs, Inc. No. 31. University, Miss.: Romance Monographs, Inc., 1979.

Lomax, Alan. Folk Song Style and Culture. Washington, D.C.: American Association for the Advancement of Science, 1968.

_____. Cantometrics: A Method in Musical Anthropology. Berkeley, Calif.: Univ. of Calif. Extension Media Center, 1976.

Manning, Steven. "Game and Earnest in Middle English and Provençal Love Lyrics." Comparative Literature, 18 (1966), 225-41.

McHale, Brian. "Free Indirect Discourse: A Survey of Recent Accounts." PTL: A Journal for Descriptive Poetics and Theory of Literature 3 (1978), pp. 249-287.

Marques, A. H. de Oliveira. A Sociedade Medieval portuguesa: aspectos de vida quotidiana. Lisbon: Livraria Sa de Costa, 1964; Trans. S. S. Wyatt as Daily Life in Portugal in the Late Middle Ages. Madison: Univ. of Wisconsin Press, 1971.

Marrou, Henri. Les Troubadours. 2nd ed. Paris, 1971.

Menéndez Pidal, Ramon. "Poesía arabe y poesía europea." Bulletin Hispanique, 40 (1938), 337-423.

Menéndez Pidal, Ramon. "La primitiva lírica europea: Estado actual del problema." Revista de Filología Española, 43 (1960), 279-354.

──────────. "Origins of Spanish Literature Considered in Relation to the Origin of Romance Literature." Cahiers d'Histoire Mondiale. 6 (1961), 752-70.

Monroe, James. "Hispano-Arabic Poetry of the Almoravid Period: Theory and Practice." Viator: Medieval and Renaissance Studies, 4 (1973). 65-98.

──────────. Hispano-Arabic Poetry: A Student Anthology. Berkeley, Univ. of Calif. Press, 1974.

──────────. "Formulaic Diction and the Common Origins of Romance Lyric Traditions." Hispanic Review, 48 (1975), 341-50.

──────────. "Studies on the Ḫarǧas: The Arabic and the Romance Ḫarǧas." Viator, 8 (1977), 95-125.

Monroe, James, and David Swiatlo. "Ninety-Three Arabic Ḫarǧas in Hebrew Muwaśśaḥs: Their Hispano-Romance Prosody and Thematic Features." Journal of the American Oriental Society, 97 (1977). 141-163.

Morwedge, Rosmarie Thee, ed. The Role of Women in the Middle Ages. Albany: New York State Univ. Press, 1975.

Nelli, René. La poésie occitane des origines à nos jours. Paris: Seghers, 1972.

Nykl, Alois R. Hispano-Arabic Poetry and its Relations with the Old Provençal Troubadours. Baltimore: Furst, 1946.

Paden, William D., Jr. "The Troubadour's Lady: Her Marital Status and Social Rank." Studies in Philology, 72 (1975), 28-50.

Paris, Gaston. "Les origines de la poésie lyrique en France au moyen âge." In Mélanges de littérature française du moyen âge. Paris: 1912; rpt. Champion, 1966, pp. 539-615.

Paterson, Linda. Troubadours and Eloquence. Oxford: Oxford Univ. Press, 1975.

Pellegrini, Silvio. Repertorio bibliografico della prima lirica portoghese. Modena, 1939.

──────────. Studi su trove e trovatori della prima lirica ispano-portoghese. Turin, 1937.

Pérès, Henri. La poésie andalouse en arabe classique XIe siècle de l'hégire. Paris, 1937.

Pesez, Jean-Marie, and Emmanuel Le Roy Ladurie. Villages désertes et histoire économique, XIe-XVIIIe siècles. Paris, 1965.

Ranawake, Silvia. Höfische Strophenkunst: Vergleichende Untersuchun-aur Formentypologie von Minnesand und Trouvérelied an der Wende zum Spätmittelalter. Mün- chener Texte und Untersuchungen zur deutschen Literatur des Mittelalters, 51. Munich: C. H. Beck, 1976.

Reckert, Stephen. Lyra Minima: Structure and Symbol in Iberian Traditional Verse. London: King's College, 1970.

Reiter, Rayna R. Toward an Anthropology of Women. New York: Monthly Review Press, 1975.

Rimanelli, Giose, and Kenneth J. Atchity, eds. Italian Literature: Roots and Branches. Essays in Honor of Thomas Goddard Bergin. New Haven and London: Yale Univ. Press, 1976.

Roncaglia, Aurelio. Poesie d'amore spagnole d'ispirizione melica popolaresca: Dalle 'kharge' mozarabiche a Lope de Vega. Testi e Manuali, 40. Modena: Istituto di Filologia Romanza dell'Università di Roma and Società Tipografica Modenese, 1953.

Rosaldo, Michelle Zimbalist, and Louise Lamphere, eds. Women, Culture and Society. Stanford: Stanford University Press, 1974.

Roubin, Lucienne. "Male Space and Female Space within the Provençal Community." In Rural Society in France: Selections from the Annales Economies, Sociétés, Civilisations. Trans. Elborg Forster and Patricia M. Ranum. Ed. Robert Forster and Orest Ranum. Baltimore: Johns Hopkins University Press, 1977.

Saba, Guido. Le "Chansons de toile" o "Chansons d'histoire." Edizione critica con introduzione, note e glossario. Instituto de Filologia Romanza dell'Università di Roma. Testi e Manuali, 42. Modena, 1955.

Sánchez Romeralo, Antonio. El villancico: estudios sobre la lírica popular en los siglos XV y XVI. Biblioteca Románica Hispánica. Madrid: Gredos, 1969.

Saville, Jonathan. The Medieval Erotic Alba: Structure as Meaning. New York, 1972.

Scharff, Arthur Bernard. "The Old French Chanson de Toile." Diss. Ohio State University 1969.

Scholberg, Kenneth R. Sátira e invectiva en la España medieval. Madrid: Gredos, [1971].

Schotter, Anne Howland. "Seduced and Abandoned: Woman as Victim in Medieval Latin Woman's Song." Unpublished paper. 1978.

Smith, Nathaniel B. Figures of Repetition in the Old Provençal Lyric: A Study in the Style of the Troubadours. North Carolina Studies in the Romance Languages and Literatures, 176. Chapel Hill: Univ. of North Carolina Press, 1976.

Spitzer, Leo. "The Mozarabic Lyric and Theodor Frings' Theories." Comparative Literature, 4 (1952), 1-22.

Steiner, George. "A Note on the Distribution of Discourse."Sémiotica, 22 (1978), 185-209.

Stern, Samuel M. Hispano=Arabic Strophic Poetry: Studies by Samuel Miklos Stern. Ed. L. P. Harvey. Oxford: Clarendon, 1974.

Streng-Renkonen, Walter O. Les Estampies françaises. Paris: Champion, 1931.

Stuard, Susan Mosher, ed. Women in Medieval Society. Philadelphia: Univ. of Pennsylvania Press, 1976.

Tavani, Giuseppe. Repertorio metrico della lirica galego-portoghese. Officina romanica, 7. Rome: Ateneo, 1967.

_____. Poesia del duecento nella penisola iberica. Roma: Ateneo, 1969.

Thorne, Barrie, and Nancy Henley, eds. Language and Sex: Difference and Dominance. Georgetown University Center for Applied Linguistics Series in Sociolinguistics. Rowley, Mass.: Newbury House Publishers, 1975.

Topsfield, Lionel T. Troubadours and Love. Cambridge: Cambridge Univ. Press, [1975].

Trask, Willard R. Medieval Lyrics of Europe. New York and Cleveland: World, 1969.

Trend, J. B. "The Oldest Spanish Poetry." In Hispanic Studies in Honour of I. González Llubera. Oxford: Dolphin, 1959. pp. 415-428.

Van den Boogaard, Nico. Rondeaux et refrains. Strasbourg. Bibliothèque française et romane, Series D. Vol. III. Ed. George Straka. Paris: Klincksieck, 1969.

Van der Werf, Hendrik. The Chansons of the Troubadours and Trouvères: A Study of the Melodies and Their Relation to the Poems. Utrecht, 1972.

Vernet, Joan. "L'origen de les liriques populars àrab i romànica." Estudis Romànics (Barcelona), 9 (1961), 1-9.

Wardropper, Bruce W. "On the Supposed Repetitiousness of the Cantigas d'amigo." Revista Hispánica Moderna, 38 (1974-5), 1-6.

Wilkins, Nigel. One Hundred Ballades, Rondeaux, and Virelais from the Late Middle Ages. Cambridge: Cambridge Univ. Press, 1969.

Zink, Michel. La pastourelle: poésie et folklore au moyen âge. Paris: Bordas, 1972.

Zumthor, Paul. "Au berceau du lyrisme européen." Cahiers du Sud. 40, Nos. 3-6 (1954), 3-61.

_____. Langue et technique poétique à l'époque romane XI-XIII siècles. Bibliothèque française et romane. Centre de philologie romane de la Faculté des Lettres de Strasbourg, Ser. C. Etudes Littéraires, 4. Paris: Klincksieck, 1963.

_____. "La chanson de Bele Aiglentine." Travaux de Linguistique et de Littérature, 8 (1970), 325-337.

_____. Essai de poétique médiévale. Paris: Seuil, 1972.

INDEX

Alatorre, Margit Frenk: 57, 78,
Alba: 82, 84 126, 127,
Angiolieri, Cecco: 10, 112
Anonymous: see Chansons de femme
Anonymous dance songs: 89-90, 139
Archipreste de Hita: 46
Ashley, Kathleen: 130
Audefroi le Bâtard: 47, 67
Bagley, Cynthia P.: 2, 81
Bakhtin, Mikhail: 11-14, 75, 141,146, 158
    Secondary intention in borrowed speech: 14, 33
    Dominant and sub-dominant voices: 12, 34, 141
    "Carnival" values in sub-dominant speech: 13, 14
    Intertextuality: 12
    "Polyphonic" periods of unrest: 13, 40, 68, 75
Bassām al-Shantarīnī: 39
Bergin, Thomas Goddard: 21
Bloch, Howard: 45, 59
Cavalcanti, Guido: 10 113-114
Cerverí de Girona: 17, 21, 23-25, 82
Chansons de femme: 1, 2, 12, 67, 94, 163, 166
    Critical controversy about: 1-3
    Heterodox values, as carrier of: 122, 137
    Sub-dominant voice, function as: 121
    Women's songs in medieval Romance Lyric:
Chansons de malmariée: 23, 98, 109, 132, and see Old French
    Lyric
Chansons de toile: 9, 34, 47, 52, 67, 94, 101, 122-3, 134-5
    and see Old French Lyric
Comtessa de Dia: 82, 84-86, 145-48, 157 and see Chapter 5.
Cummins, J. G.: 60, 67
D'Andeli, Henri: 52
D'Aquino, Rainaldo: 10, 107
D'Arezzo, Guittone: 10, 111
D'Heur, Jean Marie: 6
Dante: 11, 14, 110, 111, 121, 140, 159
Deyermond, Alan: 55, 80
Dietaiuti di Firenze, Bondie: 10
Dinis, El Rey Don: 55, 58-59, 80 125, 128, 158
Dramatic Monologue: 15
    Cerverí de Girona, "Al fals gelos": 21-24
    Soliloquy, difference from: 15
    Rhetorical appeal to audience: 16
    Theocritis, Idyll 2: 17-21
Drinker, Sophie: 89 and see Music Anthropology
Ennius: 91
Estampie: 103
Faral, Edmond: 68, 94
Faucheux, Christian: 148

Female Persona:
   Attitudes toward goverment, church, and marriage: 128-132
   Continuation of conventions in modern poetry: 24-28
   Cultural Stereotypes, stabilizing function in: 16
   Differences and similarities in five Romance languages: 76

Female Voice:
   Complement to male voice, as: 34-5, 68, 75
   Dialogical role: 12
   Fragmentation and incorporation within male voice: 34
   Poetic Function: 75
   Speech Model, as: 156

Ferrante, Joan: 86, 146, 153
Filippi, Rustico: 10, 109
French lyric poetry: see Old French lyric poetry
Frost, Robert: 12, 17, 24-27, 141

Galician-Portuguese Lyric Poetry:
   Barcarolle: 55
   Corpus, divisions of: 7
   Female speaker, persona of: 78, 128-30
   Incantation: 18, 20, 56, 59, 135
   Natural objects, use of: 54
   Refrains: 62, 67
   Texts, location of: 5-6

Girona, Cerverí de, see Cerverí de Girona
Goddard, Eunice: 140
Greek New Comedy: 17
Guinizzelli, Guido: 11
Hardy, Thomas: 12, 17, 24-27, 141
Hatcher, Anna Granville: 87, 157
Homer: 17

Italian Lyric Poetry:
   dolce stil novo:
      female speaker, persona of:
   Sicilian School:
   Texts, location of:

Jeanroy, Alfred: 1, 7-8, 34, 89, 93, 131, 146, 148, 149, 153
Khaldun, Ibn: 39
Lai d'Aristote: 52
Langbaum, Robert: 16
Lawrence, David Herbert: 17, 24-26
Le Gentil, Pierre: 53, 94
Lewent, Kurt: 22, 23
Libro de Buen Amor: 46

Male Voice: 2-3, 7, 33-34, 36, 39-40, 44, 47, 49, 51-54, 57-60, 62-63, 68-69, 75, 100, 104, 100, 121, 127, 130, 135-37, 139, 147, 150, 159
   Characteristics: 141
   Female voice, use of as complement, not foreign element: 13

Male Voice (continued):
    Fragment in two-voice lyrics, as response to female voice: 34-35
Marcabru: 44, 87, 92, 95 107, 123, 130, 157-158
Marie de France: 145
McHale, Brian: 12
Medieval History: 138-141
    Dowry customs, changes in: 140
Monroe, James: 4, 40
Mother-daughter Lyrics: 134 and see *chansons de toile*
Mozarabic Spanish Lyric Poetry:
    Arabic/Romance poem: the muwaššaha and ḫarǧa: 37-40
    Female speaker, persona of: 76-77
    Ḫarǧa as determiner of form: 38
    Texts, discovery of: 4
Music anthropology: 2, 93, 122, 132
    Women's songs in village life: 89-90
Old French Lyric Poetry: 1, 7-9, 57, 67, 93-105, 131, 134, 138
    Chanson de malmariée: see Chanson de malmariée
    Chanson de toile: see Chanson de toile
    Female speaker, persona of: 103-105
    Pastourelle, difference from Provençal: 95
    Texts, location of: 7-9
Paris, Gaston: 1, 4, 7-8, 127, 131
Provençal Lyric Poetry: 7, 21-24, 41-45, 46, 68, 81-92, 123-125, 145-160
    Female speaker, persona of: 81-92
    Texts, location of: 7
    Women poets: see Chapter 5.
Pugliese, Giacomino: 110, 113
Reverdie: 103
Rhetorical conventions:
    Amplificatio: 51-52
    Diegesis, mimesis, and the modern "mixed" style: 12, 15, 36
    Prosopopeia: 2, 10
    Repetition, incantation in female voice: 24, 56, 60, 64-65, 67, 99, 135
Ribera, Julian: 39
Riquer, Martín de: 21-22
Robbins, Kittye delle: 154-155
Saíz, Próspero: 46
Sappho: 17
Saville, Jonathan: 126
Shapiro: 146, 153-55
Smith, Nathaniel: 9, 89
Smith-Rosenberg, Carroll: 89
Spanish Lyric Poetry: see Mozarabic Spanish Lyric Poetry
Spitzer, Leo: 5, 14, 94, 174
Stern, Samuel Miklos: 4, 5
Tavani, Giuseppe: 2
Theocritus, Idyll 2: 17-18, 20, 24-25, 147
Tiddy, R. J.: 91

Took, John: 11, 22-23, 113, 159
Trask, Willard: 89, 137
Van den Boogaard, Nico: 58
Varro: 91
Voice, concept of: 3, 11-14, 33, 39-40, 50, 75, 121-122, 135-137, 158-159
   Bakhtin Circle: 11
   "Double-voiced" speech: 33
   "Secondary intention" in borrowed speech: 33
   "Polyphonic" periods of history: 13, 40, 68, 75
Welsh, Andrew: 135, 145
Yeats, William Butler: 17, 24-27, 32, 141
Zink, Michel: 94, 134
Zumthor, Paul: 94, 134